DAZZLE™

Vol. 7

Minari Endoh

HAMBURG // LONDON // LOS ANGELES // TOKYO

Story So Far...

When Rahzel's father suddenly kicked her out of the house to go on a training journey and hone her magical abilities, he didn't expect her to immediatly fall in with Alzeid, an albino magic user in search of the woman who killed his father. They were soon joined by Baroqueheat, Alzeid's associate from his army days whose arm turns into a blade, and he took quite a liking to Rahzel--much to her dismay. Yet somehow, through multiple trials and adventures, this mismatched trio formed a bond as strong as a family's ties.

But one of Baroqueheat's older brothers, Kiara, has been observing them and pulling strings behind the scenes, accompanied by a nameless little albino boy who Kiara also calls "Alzeid" (the boy tells Rahzel she promised years ago to give him a name, but she doesn't remember this). Also, Baroqueheat and Kiara's older sister Natsume matches the description of the woman Alzeid says killed his father--but she was apparently killed by an older man bearing a striking resemblance to Alzeid. Perhaps for that reason, Baroqueheat's other sister Branowen has exhibited an intense dislike for Alzeid.

Now, Rahzel and company have traveled to the town of Acanea, along with Rayborn, a teen whose life Rahzel saved. Kiara's albino companion has been terrorizing the locals, and a pair of assassins hired to hunt him down, Addy and Ashma, attack Alzeid by mistake. Even though Alzeid can usually regenerate from any wound, he falls dangerously ill from the poison Kiara gave the assassins to coat their weapons with. While Rahzel drags him to a clinic, Rayborn stays behind to delay the assassins, though he has an utter lack of magical power or other unusual fighting skill. The creativity and insulting nature of his traps keeps Addy hot on his tail, until he runs afoul of a local mob--who shoot him just because he was seen with Alzeid. The boy "monster" who Alzeid was mistaken for then shows up. Though he likes the nickname the townspeople have given him--"Silver Devil"--he slaughters them in a display of power. Only Ashma's invisibility trick keeps him and Addy safe, and they bring Rayborn's body to the doctor Rahzel found--Taylor. Baroqueheat fights Kiara to get an antidote for the poison, damaging his hand in the process, and Alzeid recovers--but the clinic has been surrounded by the local militia, who still think Alzeid is the monster...

Contents

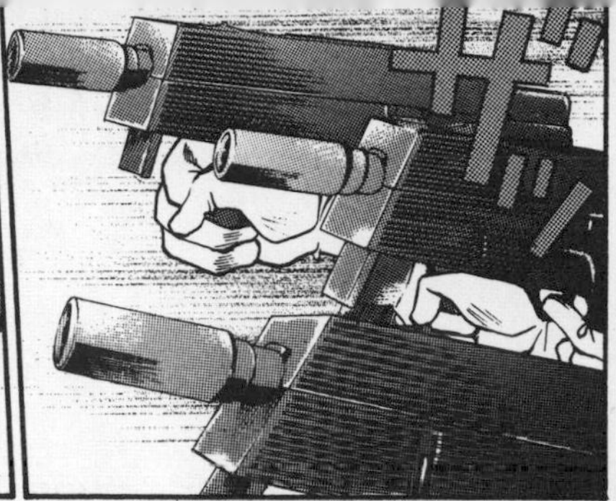

ALL RIGHT. I NOW CALL THIS STRATEGY MEETING TO ORDER.

← Still there!

ANYBODY WITH A PLAN, RAISE YOUR HAND.

HERE.

YES, ALZEID, REPRESENTING THE MONSTERS, WHAT IS IT?

Abandoning the strategy meeting
ぱたん。
Slam
I DON'T FEEL LIKE THINKING ABOUT IT, SO I'M GOING TO GO KILL THEM ALL.
GAAAH! ALZEID?!
HOLD ON-- YOU'RE JUST KIDDING, RIGHT?
DON'T GO. THERE'S TOO MANY OF THEM. IT'S DANGEROUS.
WILL YOU WAIT A MINUTE?!
creeaak
THEY ASKED FOR IT.
IT'S ONLY FAIR TO GIVE THEM WHAT THEY WANT.

Chapter 48: The Ephemeral Proposition-- Part 13: The Nature of Monsters, the Turf of the Protector

FIRE!!

URRGH!

AL--

Foom
Crunch
tinkle
DID YOU REALLY THINK THAT THE WEAPONS OF MEN WOULD WORK AGAINST MONSTERS?

THAT'S REALLY TOO BAD.

HEY!

WHADDAYA THINK YOU'RE DOING?!

MY HAND!! IT'S MOVING BY ITSELF!!

MY FINGER IS MOVING...

NO... HELP ME... HELP!

HUMANS, HOWEVER, ARE SO EASY TO KILL.

AAAACK!

WAAAH!

...!

BY THE WAY, TAYLOR.
HOW WAS RAYBORN KILLED?
HUH?
I DIDN'T PERFORM AN AUTOPSY, SO I DON'T KNOW FOR SURE...
...BUT HE HAD SIX BULLET WOUNDS AROUND HIS RIGHT LUNG.
THEN, AFTER HE LOST CONSCIOUSNESS FROM THE SHOCK OF BEING SHOT, HE WAS BEATEN.
SEVERAL RIBS WERE BROKEN AND HE SUFFERED MASSIVE INTERNAL INJURIES.
I SEE.
?!
H-HEY. WHAT'S THE MEANING OF THIS?
HEY...
AROUND HIS RIGHT LUNG...

...SIX SHOTS.
GAAAAAH!
ドサ。
ガチ
ガチガチ
ガチガチ
ガチガチ
AND NOW...

AND FOR INTERNAL INJURIES--
...THE RIBS.
?!
WHAT'RE YOU STOPPING ME FOR?
DON'T YOU WANT REVENGE FOR RAYBORN?
BUT THESE AREN'T THE GUYS WHO DID IT!
NO?
IT WAS ONE OF THEIR GANGS, THOUGH, WASN'T IT?
IF A SOLDIER IS A PRISONER OF WAR...
...DO THE GUARDS CARE IF HE NEVER KILLED ANYONE HIMSELF?
HE'D BE TREATED THE SAME WHETHER HE'D KILLED ONE PERSON OR A HUNDRED, NO?

WHO'S RESPONSIBLE FOR THE ACTIONS OF A GROUP?
HOW DO YOU PUNISH A GROUP FOR COMMITTING A CRIME?
DO YOU DIVIDE UP THE BLAME INTO TINY, PEA-SIZED PIECES?
DOES TAKING A DROP OF BLOOD FROM EACH INDIVIDUAL IN THE GROUP...
...MAKE UP FOR THE LIFE'S BLOOD OF ONE VICTIM?
THAT'S NOT RIGHT, IS IT?
THEY SHOULD ALL SHOULDER THE BLAME.
EACH ONE...
...BEARS THE SAME GUILT.

NOW LET ME GO.
SHUT YOUR EYES AND COVER YOUR EARS.
YOU SHOULDN'T HAVE TO WATCH THIS.
SUCH A BLOODY SCENE...
MY TRUE SELF...
IF YOU DON'T WANT PEOPLE TO SEE IT, YOU SHOULDN'T DO IT TO BEGIN WITH, YOU IDIOT!!
DON'T YOU YELL AT ME LIKE THAT, DUMBASS!!

IF WE USE YOUR LOGIC ...
...THEN FRIENDS OF A KILLER ARE ALL KILLERS, RIGHT?
IF YOU BELIEVE THAT, DON'T DO ANYTHING YOU DON'T WANT YOUR FRIENDS TO SEE!
STAND TALL AND STEADFAST.
OTHERWISE, I CAN'T STAND WITH YOU AND SHARE YOUR BURDEN!
—!...
clap clap
clap clap
ALL RIGHT, THAT'S ENOUGH.

YOU MIGHT THINK IT'S A LITTLE LATE TO SAY SO...

...BUT WE HAVE NO DESIRE TO HURT YOU-- NONE AT ALL.

IF YOU'LL CHALK WHAT JUST HAPPENED UP TO SELF-DEFENSE, WE'LL BE OUT OF TOWN BY THE END OF THE DAY.

IF THIS IS AGREEABLE, KINDLY DROP YOUR WEAPONS AND TURN AROUND NOW!

YOU HAVE FIVE SECONDS. PLEASE HURRY. ☆

ALL RIGHT. HERE I GO.

murmur

FIVE... FOUR...

...THREE... TWO...

...ONE...

...ZERO!!
WELL, I GUESS THAT'S ONE THING TAKEN CARE OF.
I APOLOGIZE FOR ATTACKING YOU BASED ON MISTAKEN IDENTITY...
...BUT TO BE HONEST, I FEEL PERFECTLY JUSTIFIED NOW.
IT'S ONLY NATURAL FOR US TO ATTACK YOU.
A TEMPORARY CEASE-FIRE AT BEST.
WHAT A FINE MESS THIS IS.

YOU HAVE THE SAME SCENT ABOUT YOU AS THAT MONSTER...
...THE SILVER DEVIL.
THAT'S NONE OF YOUR BUSINESS.
WHY ARE YOU LETTING THIS NO-FRAME FOUR-EYES TALK LIKE THIS, BAROQUEHEAT?
YES! IT'S JUST LIKE BEING ON LUNCH DUTY--YOU'RE ON FOUR-EYES DUTY.
UM... I'M STANDING RIGHT HERE WHILE YOU CALL ME FOUR-EYES.
IT'S YOUR JOB TO QUICKLY REMOVE ANYTHING UNPLEASANT LIKE THIS FOUR-EYES FROM OUR SIGHT, YOU KNOW.
HUH? REALLY?
WE EACH HAVE OUR ASSIGNED DUTIES. THAT'S WHAT A COM-MUNITY IS FOR!

IN THAT CASE, RAHZEL IS IN CHARGE OF BRINGING-ING UP AL-BOY.
OH, NO WAY.
WHAT THEN?
I DON'T KNOW.
I DON'T SUPPOSE BEING IN CHARGE OF CRYING AND BEING SAD WILL DO, WILL IT?
OH, BUT...
...IF I COULD...
...I WOULD BE IN CHARGE OF PROTECTING THINGS...
...SO NOTHING PRECIOUS...
...GETS LOST...
...OR SPILLED.
I WANT TO BE IN CHARGE...
...OF PROTECTING IT ALL.

Chapter 49: The Ephemeral Proposition— Part 14: And Then Quietly Ashes to Ashes

--I proposed.
WE SHOULD DELIVER RAYBORN'S BODY TO HIS FAMILY.

SORRY.
THERE'S SOMETHING ELSE I'VE GOTTA TAKE CARE OF.
--Baroqueheat replied quite plainly.

......
UMM... YOUR SILENCE IS DEAFENING.
ぷるぷる...
WHISPER
I HOPE OYSTER MUSHROOMS GROW OUT OF YOUR EARS...
IS THAT SOME KIND OF CURSE?!

THERE'S SOMETHING WRONG WITH MY RIGHT HAND.
I CAN'T GET THE BLADE TO COME OUT. I MUST'VE HURT IT SOMEHOW.
I HAD A LOOK, BUT THERE'S NOTHING I CAN DO WITHOUT PROPER EQUIPMENT.
WE'LL PROBABLY GO BACK FOR A WHILE TO THE TOWN WHERE I HAVE MY WORKSHOP.

COULDN'T YOU DO IT AFTER RAYBORN'S --?
SORRY...

I'M REALLY SORRY TO LEAVE YOU AT A TIME LIKE THIS...
...BUT IT'S MUCH BETTER THAN GETTING YOU INVOLVED.
......

IT'S MY DUTY TO PROTECT RAHZEL, SO I HAVE TO BE ABLE TO FIGHT.
I HAVE TO BE ABLE TO MAKE A DEVASTATING PREEMPTIVE STRIKE.
UNLESS I'M READY TO MEET THE ENEMY, THERE'S NO REASON TO HANG AROUND!!
UMM...
RAHZEL, WOULD IT BE ALL RIGHT IF WE CAME WITH YOU?
I REALIZE YOU MAY NOT WANT US, BUT YOU'LL NEED HELP TO CARRY THE COFFIN, WON'T YOU?
ガーン
Y-YOU WANT ME TO BE A PALLBEARER, ADDY?
THE PORT HERE IS STILL CLOSED, RIGHT?
SO WERE YOU THINKING OF GOING AROUND BY LAND? THAT'LL TAKE TOO LONG...
DON'T WORRY ABOUT THAT. I'VE ALREADY MADE ARRANGE-MENTS FOR A BOAT.
IT MIGHT EVEN BE ANCHORED SOMEWHERE IN THE INLET ALREADY.

AL-BOY, YOU'LL BE COMING WITH US, WON'T YOU?

I KNOW IT'S A ROUND-ABOUT PATH TO THAT VILLAGE WHERE THERE MIGHT BE INFORM-ATION ABOUT YOUR DAD'S ENEMY, BUT IT'LL JUST HAVE TO DO.

NO ...I'M GOING WITH RAHZEL.

DON'T.

WHAT GOOD WILL IT DO?

YOU'LL APOLOGIZE TO THE DAD, GO TO THE FUNERAL, THEN WHAT?

......

YEAH, ALZEID...

...I THINK TAYLOR IS RIGHT.

AFTER WE GO TO BERNPUELA, WE'LL BE COMING RIGHT BACK THROUGH HERE.

YOU SHOULD STAY AWAY FROM THIS PLACE.

THAT'S IT, THEN.
WE'LL ALL MEET UP AGAIN AFTER WE'RE DONE WITH OUR OWN ERRANDS.
SO WHERE SHOULD WE MEET?
HOW ABOUT THAT ONE VILLAGE?
BUT WHERE IN THE VILLAGE? WE SHOULD HAVE A SPECIFIC PLACE TO GO.

WE'LL JUST MEET AT THE INN.
NOT MANY PEOPLE VISIT THERE. THERE'S ONLY ONE INN-- IT'S ALSO A DINING HALL.
WE'RE SURE TO RUN INTO EACH OTHER.

HAVE YOU BEEN THERE?
NO WAY. I JUST LOOKED IT UP.
IT'S CALLED VELLNENE. IT'S A TINY VILLAGE IN A VALLEY.
THE INFORMATION WAS KIND OF OUTDATED, SO I'M NOT SURE HOW ACCURATE IT IS, BUT--
NOW WE NEED JUST TO FIGURE OUT HOW TO GET OUT OF HERE WITHOUT BEING NOTICED.
I BELIEVE MY WORTHLESS BROTHER MAY BE ABLE TO HELP WITH THAT.
WORTH-LESS?!

IT MEANS DISAPPOINTING, DISGRACEFUL, THAT KIND OF THING.
I KNOW WHAT THE WORD MEANS!
DON'T WORRY, I'M JUST BEING MODEST.
You know, humble.
I DON'T ACTUALLY THINK THAT, IMP.
NOW YOU'RE CALLING ME AN IMP?!
I'VE COMPLETELY LOST FACE AS YOUR OLDER BROTHER.
AND EVERYONE'S IGNORING ME!
SO, HE CAN ACTUALLY TAKE CARE OF THAT FOR YOU.
REALLY? THAT'S CONVENIENT.
YES. ACTUALLY, IT'S THE ONLY TALENT HE HAS.
WITHOUT IT, HE'D BE ABOUT AS USEFUL AS A DUST BUNNY, OR PERHAPS A LITTLE LESS.
SO, ASHMA, HOW POWERFUL IS YOUR LIGHT REFRACTION TRICK?
CAN YOU MAKE US ALL INVISIBLE?
IT'S POSSIBLE, BUT I CAN ONLY GUARANTEE AS FAR AS I CAN SEE.
ONCE YOU'RE OUT OF MY SIGHT, I CAN'T BE SURE OF ANYTHING.
TO BEGIN WITH, ALZEID STANDS OUT TOO MUCH.
IF HE COULD GET RID OF HIS SHOWY WHITE HAIR AND RED EYES, IT MIGHT BE A LITTLE EASIER, BUT...

THAT'S IT.

Tadaaa!

......

YOU GUYS ARE MAKING FUN OF ME, AREN'T YOU?
NOT AT ALL!
WE'RE ALWAYS STRIVING TO ENVELOP YOU IN A SENSATION AKIN TO MATERNAL LOVE.
YES! WE'RE AT LEAST HALF MOTIVATED BY LOVE!!
AND TO FINISH UP...
...HIDE YOUR EYES WITH SOMETHING LIKE THIS.
Ha ha ha!
......
You...
HERE, TRY THESE. MAYBE YOU WON'T LOOK LIKE SOME GARAGE BAND ROCKER.
A preppy collegiate look with
a hint of geekiness is quite nice.

WHAT THE HELL IS THIS BLURB?!
JUST LEAVE ME ALONE!!
rub
rub
hint of geekiness
JUST KEEP TOYING WITH ME, FATE!
HE SEEMS TO BE COMING ALONG NICELY.
THE WIMP.
ALZEID?
HUH?
UHMM ...
DON'T LET YOURSELF GET HURT.
DON'T EAT SOMETHING STRANGE AND GET SICK.
YOU TOO.
So after I said goodbye to Alzeid...
...I went back to the town of Bernpuela on the ship Branowen arranged.
(And was overcome with severe seasick-ness again.)

--He mumbled.

I SEE.

As we spoke about his son's death...

...Rayborn's dad kept his eyes lowered.

No condemnation.

No yelling.

Just two words. "I see."

knock knock
MR. DIORTE...
WHAT'RE YOU DOING?
YOU'LL CATCH COLD.

......
BESIDES...
...HE PROBABLY APPRECIATED HAVING YOU THERE MORE THAN SOMEONE HE WOULDN'T EVEN ACKNOWLEDGE AS HIS FATHER.
DOES THAT TASTE GOOD?
OH, YOU DON'T LIKE CIGARETTES, DO YOU?
NO.

BUT I'VE GOTTEN USED TO THEM A LITTLE...

... SINCE I'M AROUND SOMEONE WHO SMOKES ALL THE TIME.

I GUESS IT'S THE SAME WITH PEOPLE DYING.

WHEN IT HAPPENS OVER AND OVER, YOU START TO JUST ACCEPT IT AS A FACT OF LIFE.

MY WIFE WAS KILLED ALSO.

SHE WAS STABBED. SOMEONE WANTED TO GET BACK AT ME AFTER I TOOK HIS FORTUNE.

NOW RAYBORN IS GONE, TOO.

I WONDER WHO WILL ARRANGE FOR *MY* FUNERAL.

DO YOU WANT TO TRY A CIGARETTE?

ビクッ

OH!

WHAT ARE YOU SCARED OF?

DID YOU THINK I WOULD KILL YOU?

I THINK IT MAY COME TO THAT.

OF COURSE...

...I DON'T PLAN ON BEING EASY TO KILL.

I HAVE NO INTENTION OF KILLING YOU, BUT I WONDER WHAT I SHOULD DO.

RAHZEL SEEMS TO SUFFER MOST BY BEING LEFT ALONE, BUT WHAT ABOUT YOU?

HOW CAN I EFFECTIVELY TORTURE YOU?

I ***WILL*** PUNISH YOU. JUST LIKE I PUNISHED THOSE WHO KILLED MY WIFE.

I'LL PUNISH ALL OF YOU, AS WELL AS THE ONES RESPONSIBLE IN ACANEA.

WHAT?

I MAY HAVE PLAYED A PART IN THIS, BUT RAHZEL...

Ha ha ha!

SHE'S NOT GUILTY? REALLY?

THAT GIRL WILL MOVE ON AFTER LEAVING RAYBORN BEHIND.

SHE'LL GO TO SCHOOL, WORK, HAVE A FAMILY, GET OLD, REMEMBER THE PAST AND LAUGH!!

SHE'LL DO ALL THE THINGS THAT HE'LL NEVER DO, AND SHE'LL DO IT AS A MATTER OF COURSE!

THE LEAST SHE CAN DO IS TO THINK ABOUT HIM...

...SO INTENSELY THAT SHE WON'T BE ABLE TO THINK OF ANYTHING ELSE.

AT LEAST THEN...

...RAYBORN WILL LIVE ON IN RAHZEL'S SOUL FOR A WHILE.

I WONDER IF SHE'LL LIGHT THE CIGARETTE.

OR WILL SHE JUST LEAVE IT SOMEWHERE AND FORGET ABOUT IT?

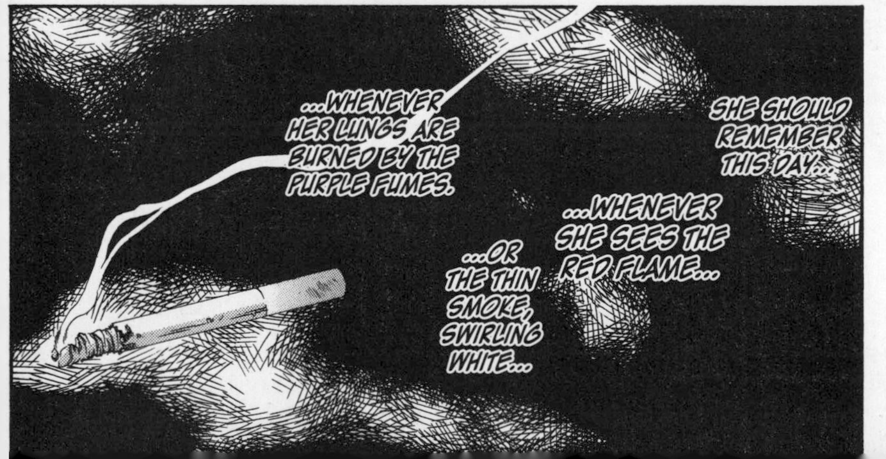

I HOPE...
...SHE BEARS THAT WEIGHT ALL HER LIFE.
WHAT SHOULD I DO? I CAN'T THROW IT AWAY.
MAYBE I'LL TRY IT JUST THIS ONCE.
NO, NO. FATHER WOULDN'T LIKE ME TO DO SOMETHING LIKE THAT.
I don't even like the smoky smell to begin with.
WANT A LIGHT?
NWAH!
NO, HE JUST GAVE IT TO ME...
I MEAN, DON'T TALK TO ME LIKE THAT!!
I HAD TO TAKE IT.
JUST GIVE IT TO ME.
YOU DON'T NEED TO EXPLAIN.

UH ...
OKAY...
WHAT THE?!
IT'S TERRIBLE HOW *YOUNG* KIDS START SMOKING THESE DAYS.
ERRRR.
......
YOU HAVEN'T CRIED.
?

......
I KNOW IT'S REALLY NONE OF MY BUSINESS.
BUT DON'T YOU THINK THERE'RE TIMES...
...WHEN IT'S NECESSARY TO SCREAM AND CRY AND REFUSE TO ACCEPT THE REALITY OF THINGS?

I MEAN, WHEN SOMEONE ACTUALLY DOES IT...
...IT'S JUST A MENACE, AND YOU WANNA TELL THEM TO QUIT, BUT--
YOU'RE JUST NATURALLY BAD-NATURED, AREN'T YOU?
YOU'RE SO CONTRARY THAT IT'S ACTUALLY REFRESHING.

NO GOING BACK.
MAKE UP MY MIND AND JUST ONE PUFF...
すうっ

IF YOU DON'T SMOKE IT QUICKLY, IT'LL BURN UP.
HUH?
O-OH.
YOU'RE RIGHT.

Cough
¥○○×△△◎⊤?!$※
OH DEAR.
SEE WHAT HAPPENS WHEN A CHILD TRIES TO GROW UP TOO FAST?
Cough hack cough

YOU'RE THE ONE WHO SAID CRYING WAS A HASSLE.
I'd have to be nice or something.
I MEANT WHEN IT'S SOMEBODY I'M CLOSE WITH.
BUT YOU'RE A STRANGER.

koff
koff
IT HURTS, DOESN'T IT?
YOU CAN'T HELP BUT CRY. IT'S A PHYSIO-LOGICAL REACTION.

SEEING YOU PUT ON AIRS AND ACT ALL STOIC IS EVEN WORSE.
STOP IT.

IT HURTS.

IT'S LIKE SOMEONE CUT A HOLE RIGHT THROUGH MY CHEST.
IT HURTS, HURTS, HURTS, HURTS.

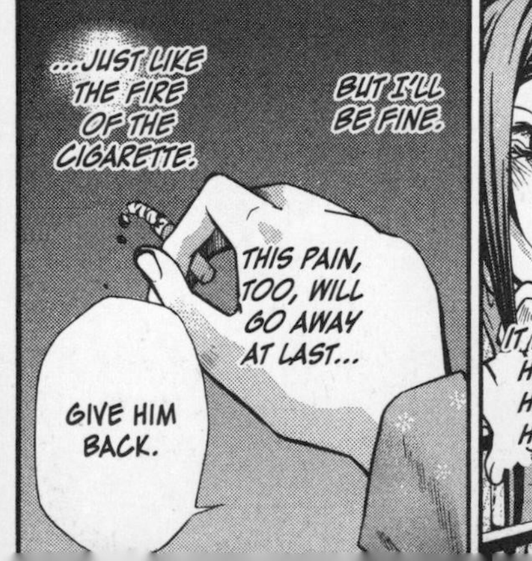
BUT I'LL BE FINE.
...JUST LIKE THE FIRE OF THE CIGARETTE.
THIS PAIN, TOO, WILL GO AWAY AT LAST...
GIVE HIM BACK.

GIVE ME BACK RAYBORN.
HOW WE MET... WHAT WE SAID...
BRING HIM BACK TO ME NOW.
...IT'S ALL BURNING TO ASHES...
IT'S NOT POSSIBLE.
...'TIL THERE'S NO TRACE LEFT.
I'LL NEVER SMOKE AGAIN.
I DON'T WANT TO ADMIT IT.
RAYBORN ...
HE'S DEAD!!

Bang!

stumble
WELL DONE.
!!
MASTER SHOGETSU!!

NOW WE'RE REALLY DONE.

ARE YOU ALL RIGHT, MASTER?

I'm bored.

VIOLIN'S NOT AS FUN AS I THOUGHT.

I DON'T WANT IT ANYMORE.

I THOUGHT IT WOULD BE MUCH MORE INTERESTING. TOO BAD.

MASTER SHOGETSU, WOULD YOU IGNORE THIS GIRL AND PLAY ANOTHER TUNE...

...TO SET A BETTER MOOD?

NO. DON'T WANT TO.

IT'S COLD. I'M GOING HOME.

THEN IS THERE ANYTHING WE CAN GET FOR YOU?

YOU LIKE THINGS! INORGANIC THINGS!

I LOVE THEM. ♡

BUT YOU TIRE OF THEM SO QUICKLY.

YOU'RE RIGHT. I WONDER IF THERE IS...

...SOME-THING I ***WOULD*** WANT--

A LIVING THING THAT WON'T BREAK OR GET BORING.

Found
drawing

Chapter 50:
Passerby A's Gloom

WOW.
WHAT A MAGNIFICENT VIEW.
BERNPUELA WAS PRETTY NICE, BUT THIS IS IN A DIFFERENT LEAGUE ALTOGETHER.
DOESN'T THE RAILROAD COME HERE TOO?
YES. OF COURSE, THIS *IS* THE LARGEST PORT IN THE COUNTRY.
YOU CAN'T COMPARE THIS PLACE, WITH ALL ITS HISTORY, TO SOMEWHERE THAT WAS A LITTLE FISHING VILLAGE UNTIL TEN YEARS AGO.

WELL, THIS IS GOOD-BYE. WILL YOU BE ALL RIGHT?

I'LL BE FINE. I WAS SUPPOSED TO BE TRAVELING ALONE IN THE FIRST PLACE.

BESIDES, I CAN PROTECT MYSELF.

NO... I MEANT SINCE YOU HAVE *NO SENSE OF DIRECTION.* ☆

ACCORDING TO WHAT BAROQUE-HEAT SAYS.

I was worried that you might not find where you're going.

WHY DIDN'T HE JUST ASK US TO GO WITH HER?

NOT THAT I'D DO IT ANYWAY, BUT--

THAT KNUCKLE-HEAD!!

WELL, YES. PERHAPS I DO WANDER A BIT FROM TIME TO TIME.

I ADMIT IT. I'M BIG ENOUGH TO ADMIT IT.

HOWEVER, HUMANS ARE ALWAYS EVOLVING.

I WILL ACCEPT MY SHORT-COMING, AND SHALL OVERCOME IT.

YOU'RE STILL LITERALLY RELYING ON OUTSIDE HELP.

NO, NO. IT'S A SIGN OF PROGRESS, OF GROWTH.

I'D RATHER DEPEND ON MONEY THAN UNRELIABLE FRIENDS.

Heh heh heh heh heh...

THAT'S DISGUSTING.

WE'LL BE LEAVING SOON.

I'M COMING.

WELL THEN, ADDY AND ASHMA.

THANK YOU FOR EVERYTHING YOU'VE DONE.

I'M NOT SURE "THANK YOU" IS REALLY THE RIGHT PHRASE.

I DON'T THINK I'LL EVER BE ABLE TO FORGIVE YOU.

BUT THANK YOU NONETHE-LESS...

...FOR BEING KIND TO ME.

RAHZEL!
But we weren't kind to you.
IF--!
IF WE EVER MEET AGAIN SOME-WHERE...
...WE'LL HAVE ANOTHER BATTLE...
...AND NEXT TIME, I WON'T LOSE!!
YOU'RE GOIN' DOWN!

WE'LL BEAT HER TO A PULP.

I'M ALL RIGHT. MY PARENTS BELIEVE IN LETTING ME MAKE MY OWN WAY.
Come to think of it, I met Alzeid and the others right after I was kicked out of the house.
This is the first time I've really traveled alone.
HUH...
I MIGHT EVEN GET A LITTLE LONELY.
No, no. Positive thinking. It's all in how you think about it.
I hate carrots. I hate green peppers.
Asparagus and beet greens should all burn in hell.
I won't have to make meals, do laundry, go shopping, or be bothered by Alzeid's pickiness...
I wish all men in the universe would blow up and disappear.
...Or Baroque-heat's sexual harassment.
Now I won't have to take care of those guys.
Traveling alone might be great! ♡
Maybe.
MAYBE?
WHOA!
WHA--
WH-WHAA--?!

ARE YOU ALL RIGHT, MA'AM?
I THINK SO.
HEY, MR. DRIVER, WHY DID WE SUDDENLY--
THIS IS A STICKUP!!
W-WHOA!!
I-I'M T-TAKING... THIS COACH.
HEY, OLD MAN.
DON'T MOVE!!
EVERYBODY... OUT OF THE COACH... OUT, OUT!!
HUH?!
WHAT DO YOU WANT TO STEAL A COACH FOR?
IF YOU WANNA GO SOMEWHERE, WHY DON'T YOU JUST HITCH A RIDE?

THAT'S MY BUSI- NESS.
S- STAY BACK !!
HMM...
すぽ
plug
WHAT'RE YOU DOING?! I'LL SHOOT!!
GO AHEAD.
WHAT ...?!

IF YOU UNDERSTAND, LOWER YOUR WEAPON, YOU PEA-BRAIN!!
I CAN'T WHILE YOUR FINGER IS IN THE WAY!!
ガラガラガラガラ
SO?
WHY DID YOU DECIDE TO DO SOMETHING AS STUPID AS ROBBING A COACH?
YOU DON'T HAVE TO LISTEN TO HIS STUPID STORY.
OH, BUT I'M SURE HE HAS A GOOD REASON.
HE LOOKS LIKE SUCH AN ORDINARY, GOOD CITIZEN.

sigh...

ORDINARY AND GOOD...

THAT'S HOW I APPEAR.

AS YOU SAY, I'VE LIVED A SIMPLE AND HONEST LIFE SINCE I WAS BORN.

EVERY DAY I GOT UP AT THE SAME TIME TO GO TO WORK. I DIDN'T DRINK OR GAMBLE.

I'VE ALWAYS LIVED A LIFE OF CONFORMITY AND MODERATION.

SO YOU DECIDED TO TAKE A WALK ON THE WILD SIDE?

WHAT'S WRONG WITH THAT? I WANT TO BE THE STAR SOME-TIMES!

I DON'T WANT TO BE AN EXTRA ALL MY LIFE!!

BEING A BAD GUY DOESN'T SUIT YOU.

YOU WERE FOOLED BY A STUPID LIE ABOUT YOUR GUN EXPLODING IF YOU SHOT IT WITH MY FINGER STUCK IN THE MUZZLE.

All it would've done is blow off the finger.

YOU DUPED ME!!
IT'S YOUR FAULT YOU GOT DUPED!
BESIDES, THE GUN YOU WERE HOLDING WAS THE COCK AND LOCK TYPE.
Heh heh

A COOK AND WHAT?
YOU HAVE TO MOVE THE SAFETY FROM THE BREECH LOCK WHEN IT'S COCKED LIKE THIS...
...OR THE TRIGGER WON'T MOVE.

USUALLY, YOU'D USE YOUR RIGHT THUMB TO DO THIS...
...BUT YOU WERE HOLDING THE GUN WITH YOUR LEFT HAND.

YOU'RE SAYING I WAS THOUGHT-LESS.
YOU FINALLY GET IT.
I SHOULDN'T HAVE STARTED OUT WITH SOMETHING AS BIG AS HIGHJACKING A COACH.

THIS IS A TOOL TO KILL PEOPLE.
IT ALSO CARVES SOMETHING IMPORTANT OFF OF YOU EACH TIME YOU TAKE A LIFE.
YOU SHOULDN'T TOUCH IT IF YOU DON'T KNOW HOW TO HANDLE IT.

I MUST BEGIN WITH SMALL TASKS...
...AND STEADILY GAIN EXPERIENCE!!
Basically a straight shooter.
OH, DANG.
HE DIDN'T GET IT AT ALL.

OH WELL. I'LL THINK ABOUT HIM LATER-- FIRST A GOOD MEAL.
Bounty of the mountain, bounty of the sea...
...agriculture and livestock producers, cook and chef, and money, thank you all for my daily bread.

Prayer

MANAGER!!

A CUSTOMER DIDN'T PAY?! GET MY GUN!!

WAIT A MINUTE!

HE'S WITH ME. I'LL PAY FOR HIM.

THAT STUPID OLD MAN!!

WELL, WHY DIDN'T YOU SAY SO SOONER?

SORRY.

OOH...

OOOOH ...

HOW DID YOU KNOW?!

DO YOU HAVE ESP? DID YOU READ MY MIND?!

I did not!

BESIDES, WHO'S GONNA BE STUPID ENOUGH TO FALL FOR A DUMB TRICK LIKE THAT?!!

slip
!!

CLUMSY!! GET UP, QUICK!!
He fell for it.
WHO THE HELL PUT THIS BANANA PEEL HERE?!!
Some...
...idiot.
STOP!!

OH, IT'S THE LADY FROM THE COACH.
THEY ROBBED ME. PLEASE STOP THEM!!
HER BAG?!

THEY CAN'T HAVE GONE FAR.
LET'S KEEP LOOKING.
IT'S ALL RIGHT. THERE WASN'T ANYTHING REALLY VALUABLE.
DON'T WORRY ABOUT IT. THANKS ANYWAY.

?!

OH...

A!!

YOUNG LADY?
A--!

THE ONLY THING I'M SORRY TO LOSE...
...IS MY GRANDCHILD'S PRESENT.

ターン
タッ
ターン
Thump
THERE!!
DON'T WORRY!
I'LL GET IT BACK FOR YOU!!

......

WHAT A PERSISTENT KID!!

GAH!!

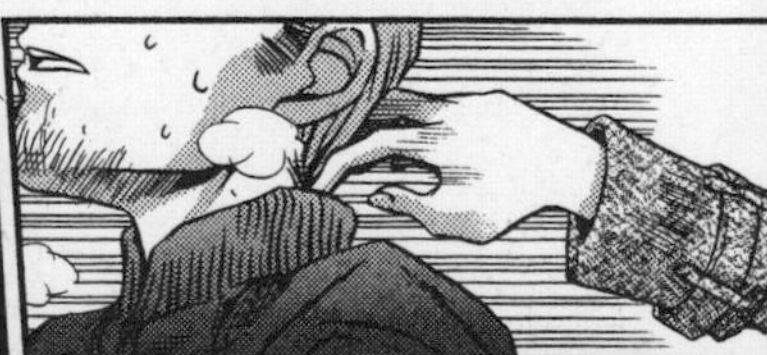

!!

HEY, YOU--STOP!!

Gasp

OLD MAN?!

LEAVE THE BAG TO ME!!

DAMN YOU! DROP IT!!
GWAH!
OLD MAN!!
DON'T MOVE!!
DON'T GET INVOLVED.
I'LL FINISH THIS.
ず!!
YOU'RE NOT GIVING UP, ARE YOU?
I WANT TO... I WANT TO PROVE THAT I CAN DO SOME-THING...
...SOMETHING THAT WILL HELP OTHERS.
I WANT TO BE FLATTERED.
I WANT TO BE PRAISED. I WANT TO BE RESPECTED. I WANT TO BE NOTICED.
I WANT TO KNOW THAT I MEANT SOMETHING TO THIS WORLD!!

DON'T UNDER-ESTIMATE ME BECAUSE I'M OLD.

YOU'LL TAKE THIS BAG...

...ONLY OVER MY DEAD BODY!!

THEN...

THEN, ONE DEAD BODY COMING UP!!

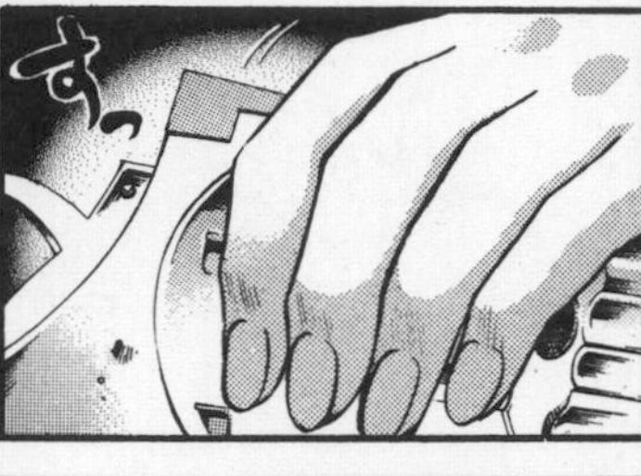
すっ

THANKS FOR BEING STUPID.
whack

I GOT IT BACK, DIDN'T I?
WELL, YOU DID MAYBE 30 PERCENT.

WHAT THE?!
くわっ
I DESERVE AT LEAST 80 PER-CENT!!
All right. All right.
WHAT-EVER.

I'M A WRECK.
YOU'RE A WRECK.
BUT I LOOKED GOOD, DIDN'T I?
WELL, PRETTY GOOD.

I couldn't find a coach, so I have to walk after all.
To top it off...
I GUESS IF YOU'RE ALONE THERE'S NO ONE TO SHOW APPRECIATION.
It's okay.
AND THERE'S NO ONE TO HELP WITH A SITUATION LIKE THAT EITHER!!
IF BAROQUEHEAT WERE HERE, HE WOULD'VE COME UP WITH A SOLUTION RIGHT AWAY.
No, no.
I would do anything for a woman.
ALZEID WOULD... NOT!!
OR SO HE'D CLAIM, BUT THEN HE WOULDN'T DO ANYTHING ANYWAY.
It's too much hassle. I'm too tired.
Sleep is always better.
THEY'RE BOTH COMPLETELY USELESS!!
A TRIP BY MYSELF MAY BE CAREFREE, BUT ONLY EVERY ONCE IN A WHILE.
I WANT TO SEE YOU AGAIN SOON, GUYS.
There's lots to tell, lots of complaints...
...and lots and lots to talk about.

AND YOUR NAME WAS...
...SAIVAH? WAS THAT IT?
LET ME ASK YOU AGAIN, WHAT IS YOUR RELATIONSHIP WITH OUR DARLING LITTLE BRANOWEN?
YOU EXPECT ME TO BELIEVE THAT YOU HAVEN'T TRIED ANYTHING INAPPROPRIATE WITH HER?
AS I TOLD YOU BEFORE, OUR RELATIONSHIP IS PURELY BUSINESS.
I TAKE CARE OF HER DAILY NEEDS.
HMM, TAKE CARE? HOW AND WHERE? WITH THOSE SMELLY HANDS?
YOU DARE TOUCH OUR FAMILY'S PRINCESS, OUR ULTIMATE IDOL OF A GIRL?!!
STOP YOUR VULGAR QUESTION-ING, YOU JERK!!
WHY DON'T YOU GUYS DROP THE SUBJECT ALREADY?

I WANT TO DYE MY HAIR BACK TO NORMAL.

AND I'M NOT COMFORTABLE WITH THESE GLASSES EITHER.

Before

After

Either way, he still looks shady.

BESIDES ...

OH, COME ON. IT'S NICE TO CHANGE YOUR IMAGE.

WHAT'RE YOU DOING HERE ANYWAY, TAYLOR?

MANY PEOPLE ARE PARTIAL TO BLACK HAIR.

STOP MAKING SLY COMMENTS !!

THE TOWN OF PROMETHEUS.
THERE'S ANOTHER, LARGER PLANT NEARER THE MINE, THOUGH, SO THEY'RE NOT AS AFFLUENT AS THAT PLACE.
ALL THE SAME, THE TOWN IS FAIRLY WELL OFF.

PROME-THEUS... I'VE HEARD OF THAT SOME-WHERE.

WELL, THEY DID SELL WEAPONS TO OBPLAY'S MILITARY IN YOUR AREA...

...SO MAYBE--

IT'S THE NAME OF A GOD.

HE CREATED HUMANS IN THE IMAGE OF THE GODS AND GAVE THEM FIRE.

......
Hmm...
WHAT IS IT?
SOMETHING'S BUGGING ME.
"IN THE IMAGE OF THE GODS..."
Chapter 51:
The Name of a Sinful God--
Part 1: The Town of Prometheus

ザー
I JUST CAN'T GET USED TO IT.
THE HAIR DOESN'T SUIT ME...
...AND THE GLASSES FEEL WEIRD AT MY TEMPLES.
COME TO THINK OF IT...
...MY FATHER ALWAYS WORE GLASSES, TOO.
THERE WAS NO ONE BUT US, SO HE DIDN'T NEED A DISGUISE...
...AND I DON'T THINK HE HAD TROUBLE SEEING.

WHAT WERE THEY FOR?

ビクッ

HEY YOU OVER THERE, NARCISSUS!

HOW LONG ARE YOU GONNA MAKE LOVE TO THAT MIRROR?

I WASN'T LOOKING AT MY-SELF!!

JUST MY GLA--

SO, YOU'RE A FOUR-EYES GLASSES LOVER?

IT'S NOT LIKE IT'S A FETISH OR ANYTHING!

WHY DO YOU INSIST ON MAKING ME OUT TO BE SOME KIND OF WEIRDO?!

HOUSE ARREST?

WOULD YOU PREFER A PRISON CELL?

IT'S ALL THE SAME TO ME. JUST DON'T MAKE ANY MORE TROUBLE FOR US.

BY THE WAY, THIS HOUSE IS VIRTUALLY IMPOS-SIBLE TO SEARCH.

IF YOU NEED ANYTHING, ASK SAIVAH.

EXCUSE ME, MISS, DO YOU HAVE A MOMENT?

WE HAVE A SLIGHT PROBLEM.

WE HAVEN'T GOT ALL THE TOOLS I'LL NEED?

THAT'S RIGHT.

WHEN I WENT TO CHECK, I FOUND THAT SEVERAL ITEMS HAVE BEEN LENT OUT.

TO WHOM?

SHO-GETSU.

THAT BRAT?

WE'LL HAVE TO GO GET THEM, BAROQUE-HEAT.
WHAT? TO HIS HOUSE?
NOT ME!!
DON'T BE AN IDIOT.
WHAT WOULD YOU RATHER DO: GO GET THE TOOLS SO WE CAN FINISH QUICKLY, OR WAIT FOR HIM TO GET AROUND TO RETURNING THEM?

NEITHER!!
DON'T BE IMPOSSIBLE.
I'LL BE GOOD...
I'LL DO ANYTHING YOU ASK!
ずる drag
ずる drag
ずる drag
ずる drag
THEN LISTEN TO ME AND BE GOOD *NOW.*

SO, YOU BROUGHT THEM ALONG?
HUH?
OH!
CAN I SEE THEM?

HOW DO I LOOK?
GOOD GRIEF!
SO HARSH.

I'M NOT UPTIGHT.

YES, YOU ARE.

DON'T BE SO HARD ON AL-BOY.

YOU WON'T LAST LONG IF YOU GET SO UPTIGHT ABOUT A SIMPLE FASHION ITEM LIKE THIS.

IT'S HIS OWN FAULT...

...FOR HAVING THE SAME FACE AS THAT MAN.

BY THE WAY, BAROQUE-HEAT.

ABOUT YOUR HAND--DO YOU WANT ME TO ADD ANOTHER FUNCTION DURING THE REPAIR?

?

ANOTHER FUNCTION?

YOU KNOW, A ROCKET PUNCH OR SOMETHING LIKE THAT.

THERE ARE PLENTY OF OTHER HIGH-PERFORMANCE, LOW-QUALITY OPTIONS.

SAY WHAT?!

LOW ANYTHING IS DEFINITELY A PROBLEM!

D-DON'T YOU DARE INSULT THE ROCKET PUNCH!!
IT'S TOTALLY COOL! KAPOW!! OR WHAM!!
WELL, MAYBE IT'S GOT A COOL SOUND EFFECT, BUT--
AND YOUR HAND SHOOTS OUT, YOU KNOW?! YOUR OWN HAND!!
I'M NOT SURE I LIKE THE SOUND OF HAVING MY HAND BLOWN OFF SOME-WHERE.
WHA--

Well...
FORGET ABOUT IT. I WAS ONLY JOKING.
OF COURSE YOU WERE!
OF COURSE!! WHO WOULD ACTUALLY INSTALL SUCH A JUVENILE...
BY THE WAY... ON A COMPLETELY DIFFERENT SUBJECT--

"HAVING DOZED OFF AT A BEAUTY SHOP, YOU WAKE UP TO FIND YOURSELF WITH A COMPLETELY NEW HAIR-STYLE." ☆
わくわく...
DOESN'T THAT HAPPEN TO EVERYONE SOMETIME?
SHE'S REALLY GONNA INSTALL ONE!!

WAIT UP, ALZEID.

I'M THE ONE WHO'LL BE IN TROUBLE WITH THE MISS.
HEY, ALZEID!!

Chapter 52:
The Name of a Sinful God—
Part 2: For Knowledge, for Capture

I forgot to draw Kotetsu this time...
But he's so small...
Yoohoo!
Where are you, Kotetsu?!

ALZEID!
HEY, ALZEID!!
BE QUIET, THOMAS.
STOP FOLLOWING ME AROUND.
DON'T MAKE UP NAMES FOR PEOPLE.
MY NAME IS SAIVAH. SAIVAH SALVARIUTO.
UH-HUH. THOMAS X SAIVAH.
All right.
WHAT THE HECK DOES THAT MEAN?
It's not all right.

IT'S ONLY MY...

...IMAGI-NATION, ISN'T IT?

......

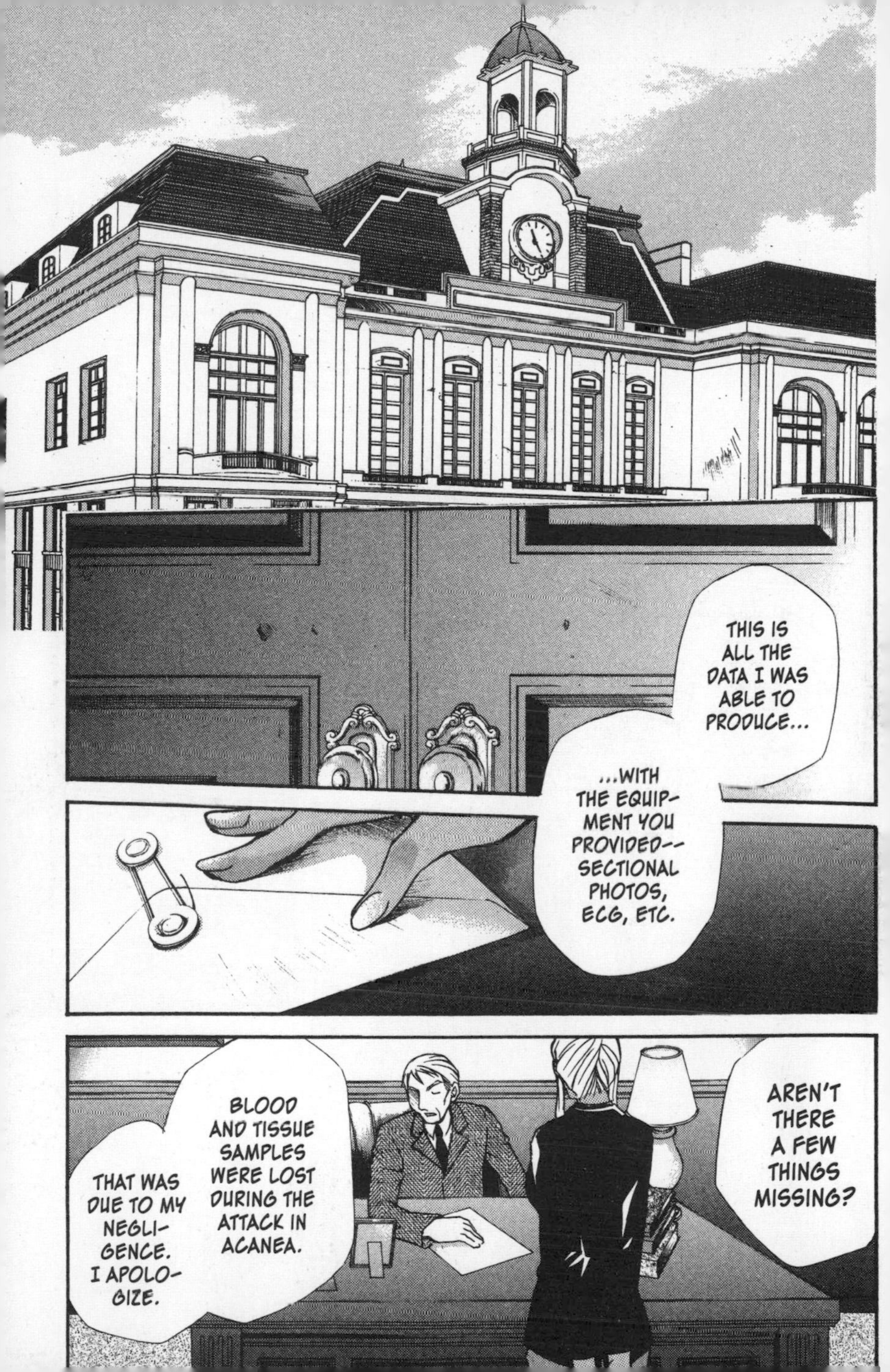

THIS IS ALL THE DATA I WAS ABLE TO PRODUCE...

...WITH THE EQUIPMENT YOU PROVIDED--SECTIONAL PHOTOS, ECG, ETC.

TAYLOR.

......

HOW DID IT GO?

WAS MR. EIZUS UPSET?

MISS KYNLENN ...

YOU DON'T LOOK VERY PLEASED, TAYLOR.

I THOUGHT YOU'D BE HAPPY AT LAST.

THOSE WERE MY ORDERS.

NOW, THERE'LL BE NO MORE QUESTIONS ASKED ABOUT YOUR MARRYING ***OUTSIDE*** WITHOUT PERMISSION.

OTHERWISE, IT WOULD HAVE BEEN THE DEATH PENALTY.

I'D HEARD THAT YOU SPOKE TO THE COUNCIL...

...MISS KYNLENN...

AMY! ♡

WELL. ♡ WE HAVE TO HELP EACH OTHER WHEN WE'RE IN TROUBLE.

I'M ALWAYS ON YOUR SIDE, TAYLOR.

THIS IS ALL MR. KIARA'S DOING.
?
I HEARD HE WAS MISSING.
HMM. I'D HEARD THAT TOO.
ANYWAY, I HEARD THAT MR. KIARA SET IT ALL UP...
...SO THAT ALZEID WOULD END UP WOUNDED AT YOUR CLINIC.
WE SHOULD BE GRATE-FUL.
BUT THE ONE WHO ACTUALLY DID THE JOB DESERVES THE MOST COMMEN-DATION, TAYLOR.
THANKS FOR THE GOOD WORK. I'LL TAKE A THOROUGH LOOK AT IT LATER.
I'M SO GLAD TO HAVE IT. I NEVER GOT TO REALLY TALK TO HIS FATHER, LET ALONE RUN TESTS ON HIM.
IT'D BE IMPOSSIBLE TO HAVE A RELATIONSHIP WITH SOMEONE WHO THINKS YOU'RE JUST EXPERIMENTING ON HIM.
NOT AT ALL! I'LL ADMIT THAT I WAS INTERESTED AT ONE TIME.
HOWEVER, HE WAS A RATHER STRANGE CREATURE, THAT MR. SECOND.
INTEREST AND FRIEND-SHIP ARE TOTALLY DIFFERENT THINGS.

AND THEN SUDDENLY HE WAS DEAD, AND WE COULDN'T EVEN FIND HIS BODY.

WE THOUGHT WE COULD AT LEAST TINKER WITH THE CHILD, BUT THEN THAT BAROQUEHEAT--

NO "MR." FOR HIM?

TO HIS FACE, OF COURSE!

SO THAT BAROQUE-HEAT...

...WAS MADE HIS MONITOR DESPITE THE OPPOSITION IN THE COUNCIL, AND WE COULDN'T DO ANYTHING!

......

UM, TAYLOR...

...MR. SECOND'S DEATH...

...THEY SAY IT MAY HAVE BEEN SUICIDE.

......

IT WOULD MAKE SENSE THAT WE CAN'T FIND HIS BODY...

...IF HE'D PLANNED IT THAT WAY.

OF COURSE WE CAN'T IGNORE THE FACT THAT ALZEID SAYS HE'S LOOKING FOR HIS FATHER'S KILLER.

WE CONTINUE TO INVESTIGATE THAT, TOO...

...BUT I JUST CAN'T BELIEVE THAT ANY HUMAN COULD HAVE KILLED HIM.

YOU SHOULD IGNORE STUPID GOSSIP.
IT'S PATHETIC IN SOMEONE LIKE YOU WHO'S BEEN GIVEN THE HEAVY RESPONSIBILITY OF A COUNCIL SEAT.
OH!
I'M JUST TELLING YOU THAT THE RUMOR'S GOING AROUND.
BUT THIS IS REALLY NO PLACE TO TALK.
WOULD YOU LIKE TO HAVE AFTERNOON TEA WITH ME? ♡
I RESPECTFULLY DECLINE.
I THOUGHT YOU'D SAY THAT. ♡
BUT YOU REALLY MUST.
YOU'RE STILL UNDER SURVEILLANCE...
...AND MUST OBEY MY ORDERS.

TEE HEE! ♡ THATTA GIRL.
MISS KYNLENN...
IT'S AMY...
...REMEMBER?
WHAT IS IT, TAYLOR?
IS THERE ANY CHANCE...
...THAT MR. SECOND IS STILL ALIVE SOMEWHERE?

THAT QUESTION HAS BEEN DISCUSSED AT LENGTH BY THE COUNCIL.
SINCE THE BODY HASN'T BEEN FOUND, WE HAVE NO ULTIMATE PROOF.
HOWEVER, IF MR. SECOND WERE ALIVE...
...HE SURELY WOULD HAVE STOPPED US FROM COLLECTING ALZEID'S PHYSICAL DATA...
...SINCE THEY ARE ESSENTIALLY THE SAME.
TAYLOR...
...THE FACT THAT YOU WERE ABLE TO CARRY OUT YOUR ORDERS...
...PROVES THAT MR. SECOND IS NO LONGER IN THIS WORLD.

THIS ...
... IS ...
... SO ...
... BOR ...
... ING!

I DON'T WANT TO DO ANYTHING.
I JUST WANT TO MELT LIKE BUTTER.
YOU ARE PRETTY LAZY, MASTER SHOGETSU.

LOUIE AND BARTHOLO WANT ATTENTION FROM YOU.
WHY DON'T YOU GO FOR A WALK?
Play with me.

I'M SUPPOSED TO BE DOING NOTHING.

EATING IS SOMETHING. IT'S OUT OF THE QUESTION.

YOU CERTAINLY DO WORK HARD AT BEING LAZY.

Ding Dong

OH! A VISITOR?

I'LL GO GET THE DOOR.

IT'S THE THIRD DAY OF THIS ENNUI PHASE, BUT IS BEING BORED ANY FUN?

I WISH YOU WOULD PUT AN END TO IT. IT'S RATHER DULL.

WELL... ACTUALLY, I THINK IT *IS* GETTING TO BE A BIT TIRESOME.

BUT YOU SEE, I HAVE A FEELING THAT SOON I'M GOING TO BE SO BUSY...

...THAT I WON'T BE ABLE TO SIT AROUND LIKE THIS FOR A WHILE.

A FEELING?

IT'S JUST A FEELING, BUT--

VISITORS FOR YOU, MASTER SHOGE-TSU.

VISITORS? WHO?

IT'S BRANO-WEN...
...AND...
AND?
BRAN?!
MOVE!!
OWW!!
M-MASTER SHOGE-TSU!!
BRAAANOWEN! ♡
MMFFFGGH!!
Erk!
YOU MUSTN'T HURRY SO MUCH!!
?!

SO, WHAT'S UP? WHAT'S THE OCCASION?
COME INSIDE--LET'S HAVE TEA. C'MON.
O-OH... MASTER SHOGETSU...
MAYBE YOU SHOULD--SHE'S SUFFOCATING.
L-LET GO!! LEMME GO!!
THERE'S SOMEONE EVEN BETTER THAN ME OVER THERE!
LOOK!!
HUH?
Push
HEY...
HEY!
BEEN A WHILE.
ぱぁあああああ
BAROQUE-HEEEAT!!
NOOO! THIS IS HUMAN SACRIFICE!!!
HOW RUDE. HE SHOULD BE GLAD TO SAVE ME.
I'M SORRY. MY MASTER'S AN IDIOT.

Eeep!
WHEN DID YOU GET BACK?
NO WAY, TWERP!
ANYWAY, YOU'VE ALREADY TOUCHED IT.
CAN I TAKE AN X-RAY OF YOUR RIGHT ARM?
NOT A CHANCE!!
THEN AT LEAST LET ME TOUCH IT.
STOP!! DON'T TOUCH THAT. CUT IT OUT!!

STOP FEELING UP MASTER SHOGETSU!!
WHAT PART OF THIS SCENE MAKES YOU SAY THAT?!!
I'M SORRY, MY LITTLE BROTHER IS QUEER.

OH? BUT BAROQUEHEAT...
...YOU'RE STALKING ALZEID RIGHT NOW, AREN'T YOU?
This is why I didn't want to come.
SO IS HE--

Don't call me a stalker.
WELL, NO, BUT--
AS YOU'VE GUESSED...
...HE'S HERE WITH US IN PROMETHEUS...

...BUT I HAVE NO INTENTION OF INTRO-DUCING HIM TO YOU ...
...OR ANYONE ELSE IN PROMETHEUS, FOR THAT MATTER.
THEN--!
PLEASE DON'T BE SELFISH.
HUH? WHY?!
MEANIE!
I'M NOT BEING MEAN.
BY THE WAY, I'M HERE FOR THE TOOLS YOU TOOK FROM OUR HOUSE. WHERE ARE THEY?
WE NEED THEM, SO WE CAME TO GET THEM BACK.
I'M NOT USING THEM NOW, SO GO AHEAD. BUT IF YOU'RE IN A HURRY...
...THEN WHY DON'T YOU JUST USE OUR BASEMENT?
WOULDN'T THAT BE EASIER THAN DISAS-SEMBLING ALL THE EQUIPMENT AND CARTING IT OVER TO YOUR PLACE?
YOU'RE QUITE RIGHT.
MUCH OBLIGED.
DO YOU NEED ANY HELP?
THERE'S NO NEED.
I KNOW HOW TO USE MY OWN TOOLS.

WHY'RE YOU PICKING ON ME, BRAN-OWEN?

Bleeech.

I WANT TO SEE ALZEID TOO.

THERE'S NO WAY THE COUNCIL DOESN'T KNOW HE'S HERE.

COULD I BE THE ONLY ONE THAT WASN'T NOTIFIED?

I WONDER WHY. THAT BURNS ME UP.

IT'S PROBABLY BECAUSE OF THE WAY YOU ACT.

NO ONE TRUSTS YOU, MASTER.

ほぎゃ

Snarl

YOU SHUT UP, BEFYLA!!

PERHAPS THEY THOUGHT YOU MIGHT TRY VIVISECTING HIM, OR GIVING HIM STRANGE DRUGS OR DOING OTHER WEIRD EXPERIMENTS.

WHAT? ON ALZEID?

THERE'S NO WAY I'D DO THAT.

Pout

QUITE! HOW RUDE!

TOO TRUE.

WHY WOULD I RISK LOSING A UNIQUE SPECIMEN FOR A MERE DRUG EXPERIMENT?

OH, IS THAT IT?

BESIDES, I'M SCARED OF BLOOD.

Couldn't possibly dissect him.

WHAT A WIMP.

BESIDES, THERE'S SO MUCH WE CAN DO WITHOUT CUTTING INTO HIM--LIKE CT SCANS AND BLOOD TESTS.
THERE ARE PLENTY OF WAYS OF FINDING OUT WHAT'S INSIDE.
YOU CAN GET INFINITELY MORE INFO FROM AN ACTIVE, LIVING SAMPLE THAN FROM ONE THAT'S CEASED ITS BIOLOGICAL FUNCTIONS.
FOR INSTANCE, IT'S SO MUCH MORE FUN WATCHING BRAINS IN ACTION ON AN FMRI THAN JUST DISSECTING THEM.

BESIDES, I DON'T JUST WANT DRY NUMERIC DATA.
LIVING THINGS AREN'T MADE UP OF ONES AND ZEROS.
ONE MUST SEE... HEAR...
...TOUCH.
IF IT WEREN'T POSSIBLE TO MEASURE THINGS WITH YOUR FIVE SENSES, THEN THERE WOULDN'T BE ANY POINT IN HUMANS GETTING INVOLVED...
...AND WE COULD LEAVE IT ALL TO MACHINES.

I'VE DECIDED.
LET'S GO SEE ALZEID.
ARE YOU SURE? BRAN-OWEN WILL BE ANGRY.
OOH, I'M REALLY SCARED.
BUT I WANT TO MEET HIM. IT CAN'T BE HELPED.
BEFY-LADITA ...
... SALA-SANEIA ...
WOULD YOU GO GET HIM FOR ME?
AND MAKE SURE...
I'm so...
... hun-gry.
...YOU DON'T OFFEND HIM.

Vellnene 80Km

VELLNENE IS 80 KILOMETERS THAT WAY.

THERE'S NO WAY I CAN COVER THAT DISTANCE TODAY.

I HOPE THERE'LL BE SOMEPLACE TO SPEND THE NIGHT ON THE WAY.

Chapter 53:
The Name of a Sinful-God-
Part 3: Let's Have a Tea-Party

THANK YOU VERY MUCH.

GUN shop

Mine-uchi

SO, ALZEID...

...YOU'VE GOT THE BULLETS YOU CAME FOR. CAN WE PLEASE GO HOME?

NO WAY. I WANNA PLAY SOME MORE.

IS THAT ANY WAY FOR A 24-YEAR-OLD GROWN MAN TO TALK?

I KEEP FEELING PEOPLE WATCHING ME.
IS IT JUST MY IMAGINATION?
ちら…
glance

....

....

HE FAKED?!

ALZEID...
NOBODY MOVE.
I WANT TO KNOW WHY YOU'RE ALL WATCHING ME.
NOT SO MUCH WATCHING...
NOT REALLY.
THAT'S RIGHT.
YOU'RE IMAGINING THINGS.
OH.
SO IT'S ALL MY IMAGINATION?
THAT'S RIGHT.
SO, PUT YOUR GUN DOWN AND--
Bang!!

QUIT MESSING WITH ME AND TELL ME...

silence

...OR ELSE...

...THIS KID WILL DIE.

WHAAAAT ?!!

THE WEIGHT OF A LIFE IS NOT MUCH DIFFERENT FROM THE WEIGHT OF A BULLET.

WHAT? NOW YOU'RE TRYING TO LOOK COOL?

I HATE TO TELL YOU THIS, BUT YOU'RE RIDICULOUS.

STOP PRETENDING TO BE SO HARD-BOILED!!

KILLING *ME* WOULD BE JUST AS CRIMINAL!

DON'T PREACH AT ME LIKE YOU'VE EVEN GOT ANY COMMON SENSE.

DON'T WORRY, YOU'RE BARELY IN THE GRAY ZONE.

IT'S BLACK! BLACK I TELL YOU!! YOU'RE BLACK AS HELL INSIDE!

LOOK! WHILE WE'VE BEEN ARGUING ABOUT NOTHING...

......
BUT WHAT *WAS* THAT, ANYWAY?
WHY WERE THEY ALL LOOKING LIKE THAT AT A NORMAL GUY LIKE ME?
IT'S NOT MY FAULT.
IT IS YOUR FAULT!
BECAUSE THEY'RE INTERESTED IN YOU, OF COURSE...
...ALZEID.
IT MAY BE NONE OF MY BUSINESS, BUT HEARING YOU CALL YOURSELF A NORMAL GUY...
...REALLY SOUNDS WEIRD TO ME.

WHO ARE YOU?

I'M SORRY IF MY PARTNER OFFENDED YOU.

HER NAME'S SALASANEIA. I'M BEFYLA-DITA.

YOU MAY CALL US BY OUR FIRST NAMES.

NO, ACTUALLY, I WOULDN'T LIKE THAT!

IT'S ALL RIGHT.

THERE'S SOME-ONE WHO'D LIKE TO MEET YOU.

IF YOU'LL ACCEPT OUR INVITATION, I BELIEVE SOME OF YOUR QUESTIONS WILL BE ANSWERED.

HMPH. SO YOU'RE JUST A MES-SENGER, EH?

THAT MEANS YOU CAN'T ANSWER ALL THE QUESTIONS.

CORRECT. BUT SINCE I AM A MES-SENGER ...

...I DON'T MAKE PROMISES LIGHTLY.

AND IF I SAY NO?

SHE TOLD YOU WE'RE JUST MESSENGERS.

WE'RE HERE TO CARRY OUT THE MASTER'S WISHES.

YOUR CONVENIENCE IN THIS MATTER IS NONE OF OUR CONCERN.

SO, YOU'D TRY TO TAKE ME BY FORCE?

YOU'RE JUST A CHILD.

A-- ALZEID?

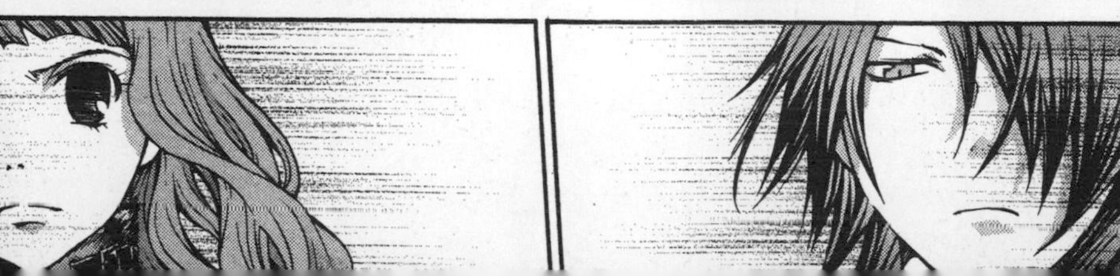

STOP IT, YOU TWO!!
YOU'RE IN A PUBLIC STREET!!
SHUT UP, BOTTOM FEEDER.
THEY'RE THE ONES WHO STARTED THIS!!
URRRGH !!

whoosh
ギン

YOU'RE SUPPOSED TO HAVE WHITE HAIR AND RED EYES. WHAT'S HAPPENED TO YOUR HAIR?
DID YOU DYE IT? HOW TACKY.
SHUT UP.

ジャリッ
EEEK!!
PLAYTIME IS OVER.
TIME FOR CHILDREN TO GO HOME AND DO HOME-WORK.
THAT'S IT.

WHAT?!
DON'T BE A FOOL!!
YOU --
TSK.

grab
HUH?
EEEK!!
YOU'LL SEE MY UNDIES!!
WHAT THE ?!
YOU PEDOPHILE!
じたばた
じたばた
LET GO OF ME! LET ME GO!!
PEDO--?!
grin
STOP MAKING THINGS UP!!
?!

DID YOU...

...LIKE THAT? ☆

WHAT IS WITH THIS KID?!

bang

TOO BAD.

YOU DODGED IT.

WELL, YOU'RE HARDLY SOMEONE WHO'D DIE FROM A LITTLE THING LIKE THAT, ARE YOU?

HEH.

SO AFTER INVITING ME AS A GUEST, YOU TRY TO KILL ME?

AFTER ALL, YOU'RE MR. SECOND'S--

A-ALZEID SAID HE'S NOT GOING.

PLEASE LEAVE NOW.

THIS IS NONE OF YOUR CONCERN. MOVE.

ALZEID IS THE MISS' IMPORTANT GUEST.

THEREFORE, IT'S MY DUTY TO PROTECT HIM.

BRAVE WORDS FOR SOME-ONE WHO'S SHIVERING LIKE A LEAF.

I *WILL* KILL YOU THIS TIME.

QUIT BEING SUCH A HERO.

QUITE RIGHT.

IT'S RUDE TO SHOOT A LADY FROM BEHIND.

CREATURES THAT CAN HANDLE A GUN LIKE THAT ONE-HANDED DON'T QUALIFY AS LADIES.

IT'S YOUR OWN FAULT FOR TAKING YOUR EYE OFF THE ENEMY.

YOU'RE QUITE RIGHT.
IT REALLY WAS QUITE STUPID.
YOU'RE RIGHT.
YES, QUITE.
BY THE WAY, RIGHT NOW WE'RE LINED UP LIKE A FAMILY OF SPOTBILL DUCKS.
YOU THINK YOU'VE WON?
I'm starting to get annoyed.
WHAT'S MY NEXT MOVE?
WHAT'S THE ENEMY'S WEAPON? THE DISTANCE?
DO I TURN AROUND AND SEE?
BUT I'LL BE SHOT INSTANTA-NEOUSLY!!
ALL RIGHT, THAT'S ENOUGH.

MASTER.
MASTER SHOGETSU!!
WHY ARE YOU HERE?
I COULDN'T WAIT ANY MORE, SO I CAME. ♡
I WARNED YOU NOT TO BE SO NAUGHTY.
WHA--? WHO THE HECK IS HE?
DIDN'T I TELL YOU TO BRING HIM TO ME RESPECTFULLY?
WELL, HE INSISTED THAT HE DIDN'T WANT TO COME.
THERE'S NOT A SHRED OF TENSION HERE.
THEN IT'S YOUR JOB TO CONVINCE HIM, ISN'T IT?
RIGHT, AL...
... ZEID --?
IT'S BLACK.
YES, IT'S BLACK.
....

S--
STOP IT!
STOP IT, YOU!!
SALASANEIA, WOULD YOU BRING ANOTHER BOTTLE OF THE SAME THING?
IT'S IN DRAWER C1...
...AT THE BACK.
WHICH CONDITIONER SHOULD WE USE?
PERHAPS BARTHOLO'S WOULD BE GOOD?
OH, I'VE NEVER REALLY LIKED BARTHOLO'S.
Ruff!!
...!!
slap
STOP IT ALREADY!!
WHAT DO YOU THINK YOU'RE DOING, ANYWAY?!!

SINCE YOUR HAIR WAS DYED A WEIRD COLOR, I WANTED TO FIX IT.

SORRY, WAS IT NONE OF MY BUSINESS?

*Note: In Japan, the combination of red and white is used for celebrations.

YOU'RE DRIPPING WET.
......
IT'S BECAUSE HE WOULDN'T HOLD STILL. HOW IMMATURE!
IS THAT ALL YOU HAVE TO SAY, KID?
WE'LL DISCUSS WHOSE FAULT IT IS LATER, BUT YOU'LL CATCH A COLD LIKE THAT.
WANT SOME OF MY CLOTHES?
NO THANKS.
THE WARMTH OF ANOTHER HUMAN BEING?
DON'T NEED IT!!

OH WELL.

GO BUY HIM SOMETHING SUITABLE.

I DON'T CARE ABOUT CLOTHES.

WHAT DO YOU WANT FROM ME?

WHAT DO YOU EXPECT TO FIND?

I JUST WANT TO HAVE SOME TEA...

...AND CHAT WITH YOU. THAT WOULD MAKE ME HAPPY.

OH, GOOD!!
...
I GUESSED RIGHT.
FITS PER-FECTLY!
I'M THE ONE WHO CHOSE IT.
NO, IT WAS ME!!
I DON'T CARE ABOUT CLOTHES.
SO, WHAT DO YOU WANT TO TALK ABOUT?
WHATEVER YOU LIKE.
YOU DON'T NEED TO CHOOSE A THEME.
YOU...
ISN'T THAT WHAT CHATTING IS ALL ABOUT?
I HAVE SOME BASIC KNOWLEDGE OF YOU, SO GO ON AND TALK AS YOU WISH.

FOR EXAMPLE, THE FACT THAT YOU WERE CLONED FROM THE CELLS OF A PERSON NAMED SECOND...

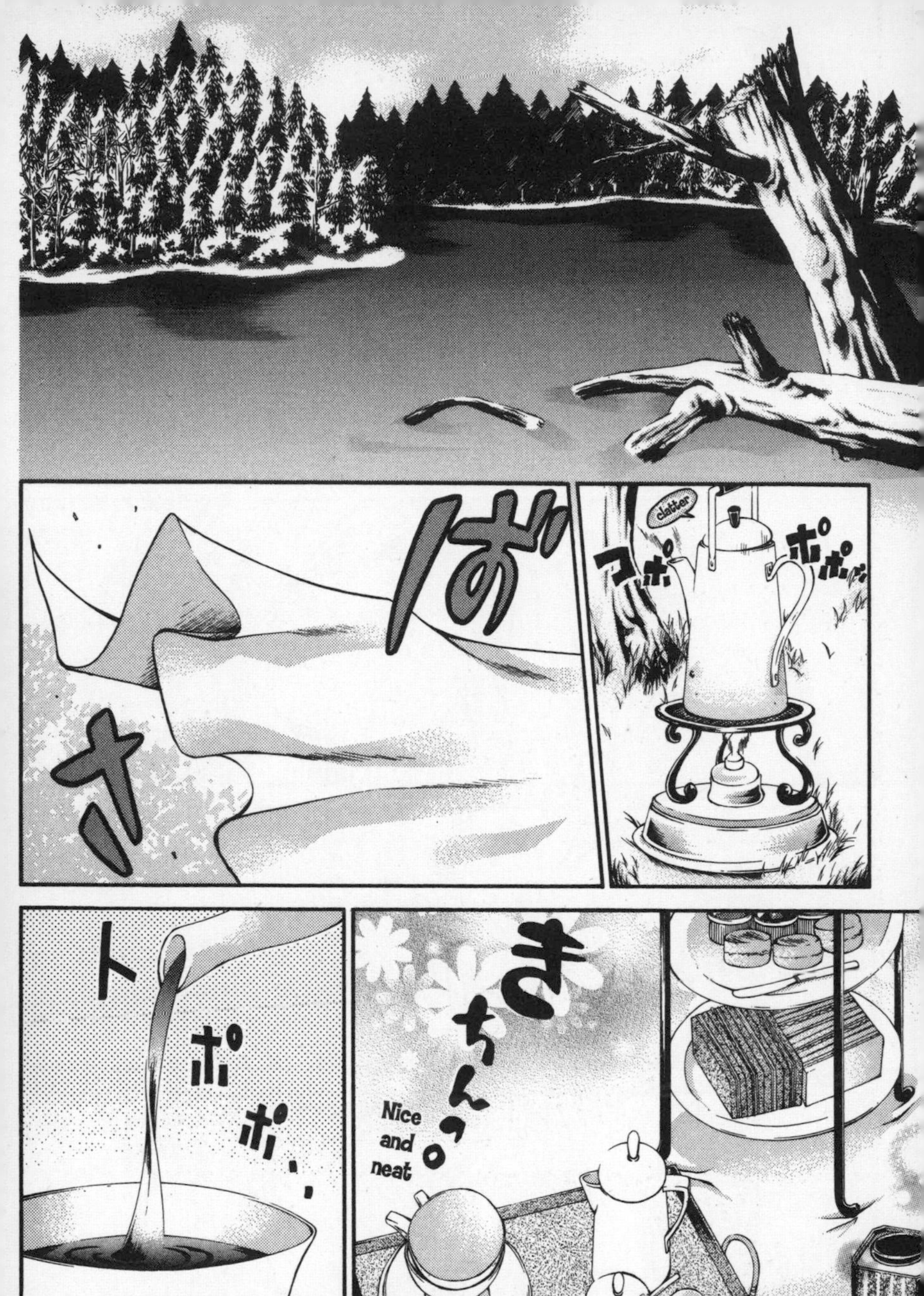

clatter
コポ
ポポ
ばさ
きちんっ
Nice and neat
トポポ、、

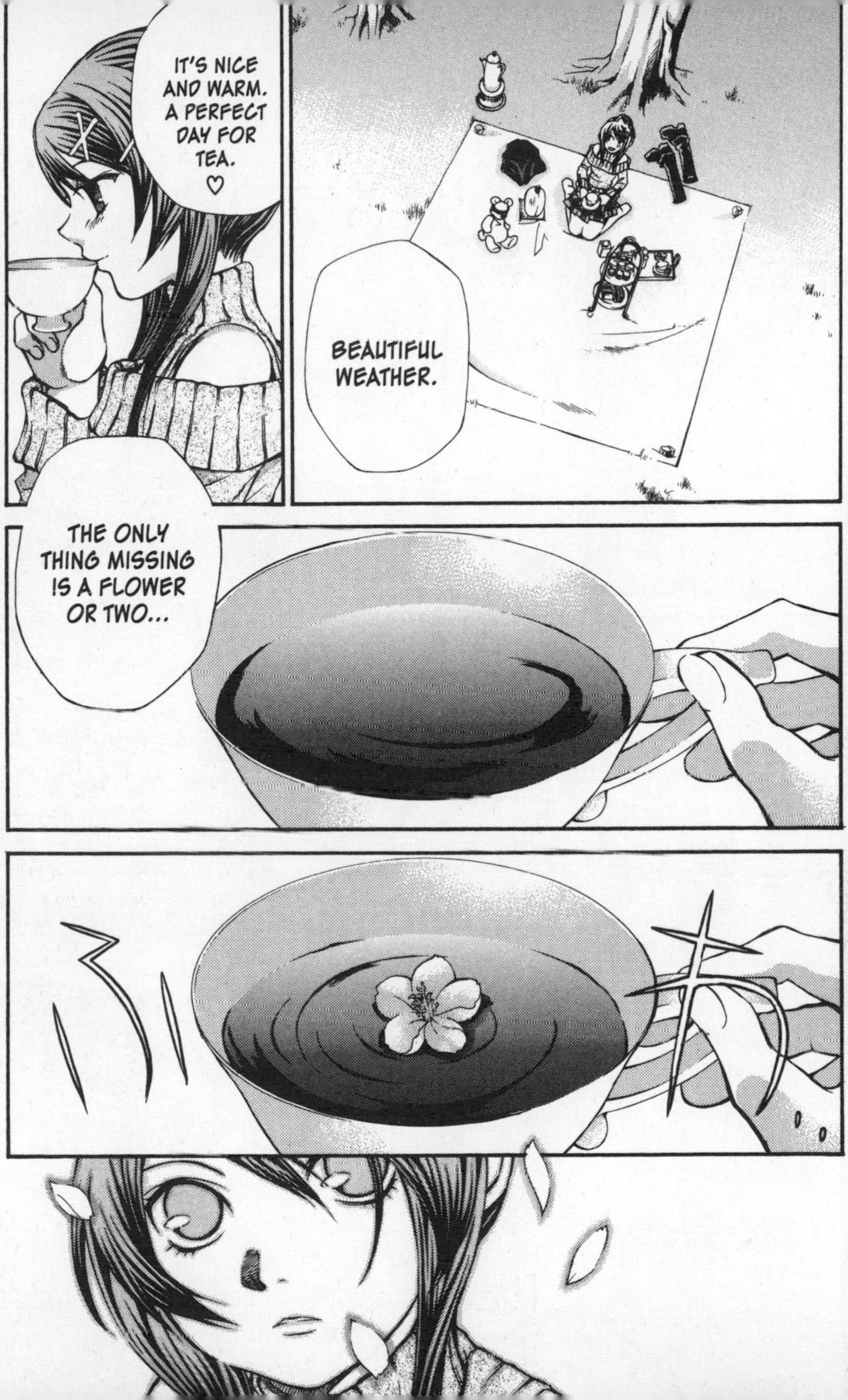

BEAUTIFUL WEATHER.

IT'S NICE AND WARM. A PERFECT DAY FOR TEA. ♡

HELLO.
HOW POETIC.
DID YOU WASH YOUR HANDS?
I BELIEVE THEY'RE CLEAN ENOUGH NOT TO CAUSE FOOD POISONING.
HOW DISAP-POINTING. YOU'RE NOT SUR-PRISED AT ALL.
I FIGURED I'D SEE YOU SOON.
IT WAS JUST A FEELING I HAD.
IF YOU'D LIKE TO JOIN ME, YOU CAN SIT OVER THERE.

I'D WANTED TO ASK YOU EARLIER...
...HAVE WE MET BEFORE?
ARE YOU SENILE?
I'D CRY IF YOU THOUGHT THIS IS THE FIRST TIME YOU'VE SEEN ME.

NO, I MEANT A LONG TIME AGO.

LIKE WHEN I WAS--

...OH, NEVER MIND.
HMMM?

ARE YOU ALONE NOW?
JUST AS YOU SEE.
HAVING A LONELY TEA PARTY?
UNFOR-TUNATELY, NOW IT'S A HECTIC PARTY OF TWO.

SINCE I HAVE AN UNINVITED GUEST.

IT DOESN'T EVEN LOOK GOOD, BUT I'LL JOIN YOU...
...JUST TO BE POLITE.

SOME-TIMES YOU SHOULD KEEP YOUR MOUTH SHUT...
...JUST TO BE POLITE.

BY THE WAY, I HATE TO HAVE TO SAY THIS ON SUCH A PLEASANT OCCASION--
DON'T WORRY, YOU'VE ALREADY RUINED THE PLEASANT ATMO-SPHERE.
WHAT IS IT? AN IMPOR-TANT AN-NOUNCE-MENT?
YES, EXACTLY.

I'M AN ENEMY, YOU KNOW.
YOURS...
... ACTUALLY.

OH.
THAT'S NOT IMPORTANT AT ALL.

I ALREADY KNEW...
...KINDA SORTA.

FATHER...
WHY DOESN'T OUR CHERRY TREE EVER HAVE CHERRIES?
WELL...
...BECAUSE IT'S A SOMEI YOSHINO CHERRY TREE.
UNFOR-TUNATELY, WITH THIS VARIETY...
...THOUGH THERE MAY BE MANY OF ITS KIND, IT WILL ALWAYS BE ALONE.

Chapter 54: The Name of a Sinful God-- Part 4: Even If We're Fated to Be Scattered About

I'M AN ENEMY, YOU KNOW.

YOURS...

...ACTUALLY.

WANT A SAND-WICH?
YOU'RE OFFERING YOUR ENEMY A SANDWICH?
I FIND THESE SCONES TASTE BEST WITH BLUEBERRY JAM.
WELL, SINCE I DON'T KNOW JUST WHAT SORT OF ENEMY YOU ARE, I REALLY DON'T KNOW HOW TO DEAL WITH IT.
BESIDES, IT DOESN'T LOOK LIKE YOU MEAN TO HARM ME IN THE IMMEDIATE FUTURE.

カチャ
IT'S A HASSLE TO FIGHT SOMEONE AT YOUR SKILL LEVEL.
IT'S NOT WORTH MY TIME IF YOU'RE LESS OF A FIGHTER THAN I AM.
I CAN.
I KNOW.
WHAT D'YOU MEAN? THAT REALLY GETS ON MY NERVES.
むっし
むっし
むっし
YOU CAN'T TELL HOW GOOD I AM UNLESS YOU TRY ME.
OH, I CAN TELL.
THERE'S NO NEED TO TEST YOU.
YOU CAN'T PROTECT A THING.
WELL, NOW THAT WE'VE ANNOUNCED THAT WE'RE ENEMIES...
...WE SHOULD INTRODUCE OURSELVES.
By the way, could you pass me the jam?
Anything but blueberry.
tear
MY NAME IS KIARA.
AND YOU?

SO, I'M BEING INTRO-DUCED TO MY ENEMY.
BUT YOU DON'T NEED ME TO TELL YOU MY NAME, DO YOU, KIARA?
YOU'RE THE ENEMY-- YOU OUGHT TO KNOW ALREADY.
Natto Jam
WELL, YES, RAHZEL.
BE MORE POLITE WHEN YOU SPEAK TO ME.

*Note: Natto is made from fermented soybeans

YOU PROBABLY KNOW LOTS OF OTHER THINGS, TOO.
OH, YES. PLENTY OF THINGS YOU DON'T EVEN KNOW.
This jam smells of destruction...
THAT SOUNDS LIKE A BAD PICKUP LINE.
YOUR FIRST GIFT WAS PRETTY THOUGHTFUL, BUT--
GIFT?
YOU MEAN THE CHERRY BLOSSOM?
IT'S A SOMEI YOSHINO, ISN'T IT?
THAT'S A HARD NAME TO SAY. I WONDER IF IT'S FOREIGN.
IT'S THE SAME KIND THAT WE HAVE IN OUR YARD.

THIS KIND GROWS EVERYWHERE.
IS THAT SO?
むぐむぐ
Sweating.
THEN IT MUST BE A STRONG TREE.
ON THE CONTRARY, IT'S A VERY WEAK TREE.

THIS SPECIES WAS CREATED BY HUMANS, BY HYBRIDIZATION, AND ONLY ONE EXISTED TO BEGIN WITH.
THEY DON'T BEAR FRUIT OR MAKE SEEDS.
EVEN IF THEY DID, THE SEEDS COULD NEVER GERMINATE.

COULDN'T THEY BREED ANOTHER ONE?
THEY TRIED, BUT FAILED.
IN ORDER TO GROW MORE, THEY HAVE TO EITHER GRAFT OR GROW CUTTINGS.

IN OTHER WORDS, ALL THE SOMEI-YOSHINO CHERRY TREES IN THE WORLD COME FROM A SINGLE TREE.
THEY'RE ESSENTIALLY CLONES--WITH EXACTLY THE SAME DNA.

NOTHING TO NURTURE. NOTHING TO CONNECT TO.
A THING THAT WAS MADE AS A SIMPLE VESSEL OF LIFE.
DON'T YOU THINK THAT'S...
...KIND OF EERIE?
THE FACT THAT YOU WERE CLONED FROM THE CELLS OF A PERSON NAMED SECOND...
...IS COMMON KNOWLEDGE IN THIS TOWN.

COMMON KNOWLEDGE?
WHY?
OH GOOD, THIS IS BECOMING JUST LIKE A REAL CONVERSATION. ♡
IT'S NICE.
SINCE MR. SECOND WAS ONE OF THE PRIMARY FOUNDERS OF PROMETHEUS...
...HE'S QUITE FAMOUS.

PROMETHEUS...
YOU MEAN THIS TOWN?
THE TOWN--AND MORE SPECIFICALLY, THE PLAN.
IF YOU'RE INTERESTED, ASK BAROQUEHEAT ABOUT IT LATER.

......
YOU DON'T KNOW WHAT TO BE SURPRISED ABOUT, DO YOU?
BUT I DON'T THINK HE'S YOUR ENEMY.
I THINK YOU CAN TRUST HIM.

AND...
...IF YOU CAN THINK WELL OF ME, IT WOULD MAKE ME HAPPY.
THINK WELL OF YOU?
ALL YOU HAVE FOR ME IS CURIOSITY ...

...SINCE I'M SECOND'S CLONE...
...SINCE I'M THE SAME HUMAN BEING AS SECOND.
きょと。
Whaaa?
BUT CLONES AREN'T THE SAME HUMAN BEING AT ALL!
THEY JUST HAVE THE SAME GENETIC INFOR-MATION.
LIKE...
きょろ
きょろ
きょろ

PERFECT!

じゃばー
Dump
?!

Wha--
WHY'D YOU SUDDENLY DUMP THAT ON THE FLOOR?!
? THE STUFF INSIDE WAS IN THE WAY, SO I JUST POURED IT OUT.
THAT'S NOT WHAT I MEAN!!

PLEASE DON'T MIND HIM. THE MASTER'S ALWAYS LIKE THAT.
YOU'RE NOT VERY SPONTAN-EOUS, ARE YOU?
YOU KNOW ABOUT IDENTICAL TWINS, DON'T YOU?
A SINGLE FERTILIZED EGG, BEFORE IT IMPLANTS IN THE UTERUS...
...SPLITS INTO TWO SEPARATE ENTITIES...
...AND BECOMES TWINS.

THEY BOTH HAVE THE SAME GENETIC INFOR-MATION...
LET'S SAY THAT WHAT'S INSIDE THIS TEAPOT IS THE FERTILIZED EGG.
...JUST LIKE CLONES.

THE TWINS THAT ARE BORN ARE LIKE THESE CUPS OF TEA.
THE CONTENTS ARE EXACTLY THE SAME.

BUT IF THE CUPS ARE DIFFERENT TEMPERATURES BEFORE I POUR, THE TEMPERATURE OF THE TEA WILL ALSO BE DIFFERENT.

......

THE TEA THAT'S IN THE CUP THAT I POURED OUT BEFORE IS A LITTLE BIT WARMER.

IT WAS SUPPOSED TO BE EXACTLY THE SAME, BUT THERE'S ALREADY A DIFFERENCE IN TEMPERA-TURE.

THAT'S AN ENVIRON-MENTAL DIFFER-ENCE.

YOU CAN'T GET AWAY FROM THEM.

HAVE THE WARMER ONE.

IT'S ALL BUNK.

TEA IS TEA.

ONE...TWO... WHAT?! HOW MANY TEASPOONS OF SUGAR IS THIS GUY GONNA DUMP IN HIS TEA?

THREE... FOUR... FIVE?!

YOU'RE RIGHT.

YOU PUT IN SUGAR AND MILK.

BUT YOUR MILK TEA AND MY STRAIGHT TEA...
...ARE THEY THE SAME?
IDENTICAL TWINS AND CLONES HAVE THE SAME DNA...
...BUT THEY DON'T EVEN LOOK EXACTLY THE SAME ON THE OUTSIDE.
THEIR FINGER-PRINTS ARE DIF-FERENT...
...AND THEIR VOICES, TOO.
OR TAKE BOY AND GIRL IDENTICAL TWINS.
BY CONVENTIONAL WISDOM THEY CAN'T EXIST, BUT THEY DO IN REALITY.

HERE'S ANOTHER EXAMPLE, ALZEID...
DO THESE TWO LOOK LIKE THE SAME PERSON?
?
WE WERE MADE FROM THE EXACT SAME CELLS.
THEY TINKERED WITH US LATER...
...BUT GENETICALLY SPEAKING, WE'RE CLONES.
HEE HEE. DID YOU THINK YOU WERE SO SPECIAL?
TOO BAD. WE'RE ALSO MAN-MADE CREATURES...
...THE SAME AS YOU.

......
WH- WHAT'RE YOU LOOKING AT?!! IT'S NOTHING SPECIAL.
BESIDES, LOOK AROUND YOU. THERE'S A BUNCH--
THIS IS WHERE TEATIME ENDS.
I THOUGHT I TOLD YOU NOT TO GO OUTSIDE, ALZEID.
AND...
...I DID NOT GIVE YOU PERMISSION TO MEET WITH HIM...
... SHO-GETSU.

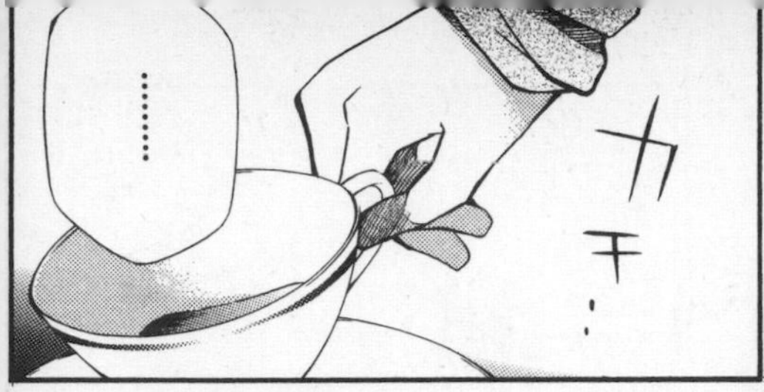
......
カチ

ALZEID?
ス

WHAT?! ARE YOU ALREADY GOING HOME? ALZEID?
YEAH. THANKS FOR THE TEA.

WE WILL TAKE OUR LEAVE AS WELL.

THANKS FOR YOUR HOSPITALITY.

WE'LL PAY YOU BACK SOMETIME.

ぱたん。

AWWW...

DID I DETECT SARCASM?

DEFINITELY.

LET'S TALK--

WHAT COULD I POSSIBLY HAVE TO SAY TO YOU?

WHATEVER COMES TO YOUR MIND, **AS** IT COMES TO YOUR MIND.

THEN LET ME ASK YOU...

...ARE YOU FROM THIS TOWN?

YES.

AND THEN AGAIN, NO.

......

ARE YOU MESSING WITH ME ALREADY?

HEAVENS, NO.

FIRST OF ALL, I WASN'T BORN HERE...

...AND I DON'T HAVE A HOUSE HERE EITHER.

BUT IF YOU MEAN AM I CONNECTED TO PROMETHEUS IN SOME WAY, I WOULD HAVE TO SAY YES.

THAT'S A COP-OUT. NEXT...

...IS IT TRUE THAT MY FATHER LIVED IN THIS TOWN?

IF SO, WHY DID HE LEAVE?

THE ANSWER IS YES.

AND HE LEFT BECAUSE HE KILLED A WOMAN.

HE VISITED PROMETHEUS OCCASIONALLY AFTERWARD...

...BUT WHY HE DID IT, NOBODY WILL EVER KNOW.

BAROQUE-HEAT...

...DID YOU KNOW MY FATHER?

YES.
WHAT ARE YOU AFTER?
WHAT ARE YOU PLANNING BEHIND THAT CARELESS GRIN?!
...I'M SORRY.

I'M GOING BACK.

HE'S GOING AHEAD.

DOES HE HAVE THE KEY TO YOUR PLACE, BRAN?

NO WAY.

He knows Alzeid too well.

Whoa!

WAIT, ALZEID! DON'T BREAK ANY WINDOWS OR ANYTHING TO GET INSIDE!!

YOU'RE A FOOL.
A FOOL?
A HELPLESS FOOL.
YOU'VE SPOILED YOUR TRUST AND SOILED YOUR PRIDE.
I CAN'T BELIEVE THAT THIS IS STILL WORTH CARRYING OUT AFTER ALL THE OPPOSITION YOU'VE EN-COUNTERED.
I'M SORRY.
I JUST CAN'T BELIEVE IT.
OH DEAR.
BUT I DO KNOW...
...HOW MUCH EMOTION YOU MUST SILENCE...
...IN ORDER TO BE AROUND ALZEID--
--A PERSON WITH THE SAME FACE...
...AS THE MAN WHO KILLED OUR NATSUME.

THEY DON'T BEAR FRUIT...
...OR MAKE SEEDS.
NOTHING TO NURTURE. NOTHING TO CONNECT TO.
A THING THAT WAS MADE AS A SIMPLE VESSEL OF LIFE.
DON'T YOU THINK THAT'S KIND OF EERIE?

THEY STILL FLOWER EVERY YEAR.

EVEN IF ALL THEY DO IS SCATTER THEIR PETALS...
...THEIR BEAUTY MAKES MY HEART ACHE.
HEY, FATHER.
MAYBE THE REASON THERE'S SO MANY FLOWERING CHERRY TREES, EVEN THOUGH THEY CAN'T REPRODUCE NATURALLY...
...IS BECAUSE SO MANY PEOPLE WANTED THEM.
I...
...LIKE THEM.
DON'T WORRY.
THEY'RE NOT LONELY.
THEY'RE WANTED. THEY'RE LOVED.
THEY'RE NOT ALONE.

GLOOMY ...
--I MEAN, NOT ME, BUT OUTSIDE.
I WONDER WHAT TIME IT IS.
I'M...
... HUNGRY.
knock
knock
knock
AL-BOY, DIN-DIN.
AREN'T YOU HUNGRY?
OPEN THE DOOR, WILL YOU?
Din-din?
Is he ignoring me?

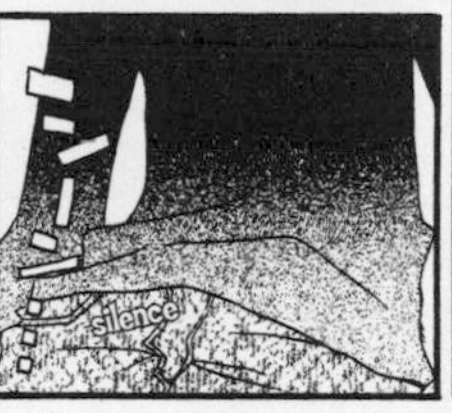

NO WAY, JOSÉ. ☆

LET GO.

NOT GONNA HAPPEN! ☆

LET GO.

WHILE YOU SIT THERE...
...AND EAT YOUR DINNER, CAN I TALK TO YOU?
AYE-AYE.
I TOLD YOU ABOUT THE WOMAN WHO TATTOOED MY HAND, DIDN'T I?
IN EXCHANGE, SHE MADE ME PROMISE TO CARRY OUT HER LAST WISHES.
CAN YOU BELIEVE THERE WERE THREE?! SHE WAS SUCH A PUSHY BROAD.
WELL, I WAS IN LOVE WITH HER AND STUFF, SO...

THE FIRST ONE WAS: HELP ALZEID.
SO I HAVE TO DO IT.
IS THAT WHY YOU APPROACHED ME?
UH-HUH.
WAS THAT AFTER YOU JOINED THE OBPLAY ARMY?
NO, LONG BEFORE THAT.
ABOUT THE TIME YOU LEFT HOME AFTER YOU LOST YOUR PARENTS.
YOU WERE A LITTLE CHILD.
HEY, WAIT. HOW OLD DID YOU SAY YOU WERE?
TWENTY-EIGHT! AT THE HEIGHT OF MY MANHOOD.
OH, HOW DARE YOU?!
SO YOU'VE LIED ABOUT YOUR AGE, AND YOU'VE BEEN STALKING ME? YOU'RE A TOTAL CRIMINAL.
I ONLY STALK RAHZEL, NOT YOU.

AFTER SAYING THAT, I'M SUDDENLY FILLED WITH SADNESS.

OH NO. I'M OUT OF RAHZEL ENERGY. I HAVE NO MORE POWER LEFT IN ME...

vween

empty

max

Rahzel-o-meter

WHAT THE HELL DID YOU WANT TO TALK ABOUT, ANYWAY?!

IF YOU LIKE THAT KID SO MUCH, WHY DON'T YOU LEAVE ME THE HELL ALONE AND GO AFTER HER?!!

DON'T BE SUCH A PARTY POOPER.

WE'RE ALL FRIENDS, AREN'T WE?

FRIENDS ?!!

DON'T TAKE ME FOR AN IDIOT!!

SORRY, BUT THAT'S THE WAY I FEEL.

I HOPE EVEN NOW THAT WE CAN GO ON...

...TRAVELING TOGETHER WITH RAHZEL.

YOU ARE...
...A COWARD...
I KNOW.
...AND A BASTARD.
I KNOW.
I KNOW DAMN WELL.
I'M SORRY.

URRRGH! WHAT DO YOU THINK YOU'RE DOING?!

THE TEA PARTY'S OVER. GOOD-BYE.

DON'T FOLLOW ME AROUND.

I JUST HAPPEN TO BE GOING IN THE SAME DIRECTION, THAT'S ALL.

YOU'RE SO CONCEITED.

WELL, I MEAN...
...JUST STOPPING BY?
?
I'M SUPPOSED TO MEET MY FRIENDS IN VELLNENE...
...BUT SINCE I DON'T WANT TO BE THERE, I'M TAKING MY TIME.
YOU DON'T WANT TO SEE YOUR FRIENDS?
NO, I JUST DON'T LIKE THAT PLACE.
SINCE I DON'T WANT TO BE THERE LONG, I'M KILLING TIME!!
THAT WAY, IF THEY HAPPEN TO GET THERE BEFORE ME, WE CAN LEAVE AS SOON AS WE MEET UP.

WHY'RE YOU TELLING YOUR TROUBLES TO YOUR ENEMY?
WHY DON'T YOU TELL YOUR FRIENDS?
I'M TALKING TO MYSELF.
I CAN'T HELP IT, AND I CAN HARDLY TELL THEM NOW.

EVEN THOUGH THEY'RE YOUR FRIENDS?
IS THAT SO?
THERE ARE SOME WEAKNESSES THAT YOU JUST DON'T WANT YOUR FRIENDS TO KNOW ABOUT.
OH, YOU DON'T WANT ANY COMMENTS, SINCE YOU'RE TALKING TO YOURSELF, RIGHT?

QUITE RIGHT.
QUITE.

SINCE YOU'RE MY ENEMY.
I AM YOUR ENEMY.

...IF YOU KEEP GOING THIS WAY, YOU SHOULD SEE SOME LIGHTS SOON.
ON THE WAY, THE ROAD FORKS TO THE RIGHT...
...BUT DON'T TURN THAT WAY.

NOW...

IT'S NONE OF YOUR BUSINESS WHERE I TURN.
SO, IS THIS GOOD-BYE?
THAT'S RIGHT.

THIS IS IT FOR BEING NICE.

CAN'T YOU SAY SOMETHING NICE EVEN IN FAREWELL?

NEXT TIME I SEE YOU, I'LL HURT YOU.
IF YOU DON'T WANT TO DIE, GET STRONG QUICKLY, RAHZEL.
Idiot!
OR SHOULD I SAY...

...RAHZËNSHIA ROSE.

HOW?
HOW DO YOU KNOW THAT NAME?!
MAYBE BECAUSE I'M YOUR ENEMY?
DON'T EVADE THE QUES-TION!!

SINCE...

I *HAVE* SEEN YOU BEFORE!!

I CAN'T REMEMBER NOW--NOT RECENTLY, BUT A LONG, LONG TIME AGO.

I *KNOW* I'VE SEEN YOU BEFORE!!

WHY HAVE I FORGOTTEN?

IT'S PART OF SOMETHING VERY IMPORTANT!

SEE YA, RAHZEL.

Remember, keep going straight, you directionless idiot.

I won't forgive you if you dare make a right turn, you dumb little hog!!

Flashback

OKAY !!

MASTER...
...THE PACKAGE YOU'VE BEEN WAITING FOR IS HERE.
THANKS.
AND WHAT'S THIS?
IF YOU WANT MORE DETAILED INFORMATION, THEY SAID TO REQUEST IT OFFICIALLY.
NOT EVERYONE HAS AS MUCH FREE TIME AS YOU, MASTER.
WHAT IS THAT, MASTER SHO-GETSU?
I'LL SHOW IT TO YOU LATER IF YOU WANT.
OH, IT'S A WOMAN.
WOMAN ?!
WHAT'S THE MEANING OF THIS, BEFYLA ?!!
WHY TAKE IT OUT ON ME?
I ASKED FOR INFORMATION ABOUT ALZEID'S DAILY LIFE...
...AND IT SEEMS THAT THERE'S A WOMAN TRAVELING WITH HIM.

IT DOESN'T INDICATE HER AGE OR APPEARANCE, BUT... HUH? THERE'S A NOTE...

IS SHE PRETTY?!!

I CAN'T TELL. THERE'RE NO PICTURES.

HMMM. IT SEEMS SHE'S A WITCH.

SINCE THEY WENT TO THE TROUBLE OF MAKING A NOTE...

...IT CAN'T JUST BE BENDING SPOONS OR GUESSING THE RIGHT CARD.

HOW GREAT! HOW FUN!

Pout

DOES SHE INTEREST YOU?

OF COURSE! VERY MUCH!

CAN YOU BELIEVE THAT SUCH A RARE CHARACTER IS WITH THE TWO OF THEM?!

IT'S LIKE A DUCK IS PARADING WITH A CLAY POT AND MOUNTAIN DELICACIES!

I WONDER ABOUT THAT EXPRESSION...

*Note: This is like saying there's a turkey walking around holding a roasting pan and some stuffing.

MY INTUITION'S ALWAYS RIGHT.

HEH...

フラ...

HEH HEH HEH.

chirp

chirp

I...

...DID IT!!

SEE? I GOT TO THE VILLAGE OKAY!
SOMETHING THAT LOOKS REMARKABLY LIKE THE MORNING SUN IS RATHER BRIGHT, BUT THAT'S NOT MUCH OF A PROBLEM.
sun
sun
sun
I'M SO GLAD I DIDN'T LISTEN TO THAT STUPID STALKER.
I kinda feel like a vampire or something.

ALL RIGHT! I'LL CHECK WHERE WE ARE NOW...
HMMM... TRIDENN, IS IT? THE NAME OF THIS VILLAGE...
Tridenn
Meeew! Pay the toll.
Give me fishies! Meow. meow.
FROM HERE, PROMETHEUS, WHERE ALZEID WENT...
...IS CLOSER THAN VELLNENE.

UHMM, TRIDENN, TRIDENN...
...HUH?

I WONDER IF BAROQUE-HEAT'S ARM HAS BEEN REPAIRED YET.
By the way, you should stop...
...imagining us in flashbacks like this.
It's kind of creepy.
I WONDER IF IT'S MIRACULOUSLY TAKING A LONG TIME TO FIX, AND THEY HAVEN'T LEFT YET.
WOULD IT BE POSSIBLE TO MEET UP THERE?

BUT...

EVEN IF WE MISS ONE ANOTHER...

...AT LEAST I WOULDN'T HAVE TO WAIT FOR THEM IN VELLNENE.

MAYBE I'LL GO TO PROMETHEUS.

Dazzle Volume 7 END

Editor
Yosuke Sugino

Staff
Kaori Komori
Alice Tsukada
Shuko Yonemoto

Chapter 48: The Nature of Monsters, the Turf of the Protector

A chapter of Alzeid's mass murder. I drew lots of blood on the ground, but I guess it was difficult to tell what it was before coloring it in. One of my lady assistants said, "What? This is blood? I thought it was cerebral fluid." "Me too." "Me too." They kept making biting comments about it. Even though I'm writing this manga, I actually hate anything that splatters. I've never watched a splatter film. I even get teary-eyed when I cut off the head of a fish. I'm a real chicken--I wish I could rid the world of all roller coasters and horror films.

Chapter 49: And Then Quietly Ashes to Ashes

The is the final chapter of the Ephemeral Proposition (you all call it Rayborn's episode--me too), and the ending scene with the cigarette was the first part I thought of. It took me four years since getting that idea to arrive here, but by this point, I almost didn't care if I ever drew this scene. I don't want Rayborn to be dead. Can't something be done? Hey? I've been thinking about this throughout the series. I've been asking myself why I care so much about an imaginary person. I've been noncommittal for a long time.

Well, in the end, he's still just a cute young boy.

Chapter 50: Passerby A's Gloom

It's the fiftieth chapter. How great! Good job, me! Thank you, everyone!! Please keep up the good work!!

Chapter 51: The Town of Prometheus

Since Alzeid looked so bad with black hair, we had a hard time remembering to color his hair. So that we wouldn't forget, I remember writing in stuff like, "color!" (you're right), "black hair!" (easily understood), "kind of black!" (what is?), "fake!" (don't know what's going on). Why was there was always an exclamation point at the end? I want to ask my past self the same question.

Chapter 52: For Knowledge, for Capture

I was so happy that I got to draw lots of Shogetsu. It's love. He's my pet. I was constantly complaining that his hair was so difficult to draw, but he's still my favorite. He's so cute. My coloring assistant kept asking me, "Don't you want to change his hair? Maybe go bold?" But he's still a cutie.

I mean, don't ask the impossible.

Chapter 53: Let's Have a Tea Party

I'm no good at drawing battle scenes. If I were asked what I'm good at, I'd have to say--I'm not good at anything, but battle scenes are the worst. I'm so bad at it that when I submit the rough drafts to my editor, I often omit the action scenes, which really makes no sense at all.

On another note, Alzeid is getting crazy beyond my wildest dreams. In the fourth volume he got saved by a girl, then in the last volume he got carried by a girl, and now he seriously fights a girl with a machine gun. This is a most improbable hero.

Chapter 54:
Even If We're Fated to Be Scattered About

I think Kiara is a very kind, good child. In the end, he eats what's given to him, brings gifts... Oh, by the way, sorry. In her profile in Volume 1...

I got Rahzel's weight wrong.

At that weight she would be skin and bones! The correct weight is 48 kg, and even that is quite light. Her height and weight are the same as my friend's. He's small, but a real fighter. After years of training, he has only seven percent body fat. There are only three kilograms of fat on his body.

I was finally able to publish the second limited edition calendar as promised. All thirteen illustrations are fresh off the drawing board. They made a CD this summer too, and I feel like I'm living off the fruits of somebody else's labors in a big way. This is the fifth year of Dazzle. No wonder I'm getting old. Suddenly, I'm older than Alzeid, too.

Thanks to all of you who have cheered me on and supported me. Thank you very much. I love you all. I hope you'll all continue to give me support in the future.

Minari Endoh
遠藤海成

Bonus Dazzle
BRAAAN-SAAAN.
HELLO... WE CAME TO PLAY.
N--
NO WAY! GO HOME!!
OH, COME ON. DON'T BE SUCH A PARTY POOPER.
I EVEN BROUGHT YOU A SPECIAL, FANCY GIFT.
DON'T WANT IT!!
YOU THINK I'D BE SWAYED BY SOME MATERIAL THING, YOU IMP?!!
BUT I MADE IT MYSELF!

Emer gency!
IT'S A SUPER-ALLOY MECHA KOTETSU.
PLEASE ACCEPT IT!!
MECHA...
...KOTETSU?!
UMM... WELL... MECHA... I MEAN...
WHAT?! ARE YOU TRYING TO OUTDO ME?!
I'M SORRY, THE MASTER'S AN IDIOT.
IT COMES NICELY EQUIPPED WITH A ROCKET PUNCH & A NUCLEAR REACTOR--STANDARD!!
NUCLEAR REACTOR...
UMM... ERR... THAT IS...

This is the poster
from volume one.

This is the original first page of volume one.

In the next Dazzle!

Rahzel and company's journey to Vellnene, the town with blue-eyed, black-haired residents where Alzeid hopes to gather clues about his father's killer, finally reaches its goal--but will he like the answers he finds? And why was Rahzel so reluctant to go there? The truth behind the night Rahzel was abandoned in the woods as a child is finally revealed--and at long last, Rahzel's father shows his face!

FOR MORE INFORMATION VISIT: WWW.TOKYOPOP.COM

Follow the MAGICAL and MYSTERIOUS adventures of Mikan at the Alice Academy!
Young Mikan runs away to Tokyo after her best friend is transferred to an exclusive and secretive private school for geniuses. But there is more to Alice Academy than meets the eye—it is actually home to children with special powers. If Mikan wants to stay by her friend's side—and stay *alive*—she must discover the Alice that lives within her!
TOKYOPOP
Gakuen ALICE
A
TACHIBANA HIGUCHI
1
The huge, new series from Japan with more than
3 MILLION BOOKS SOLD!
FANTASY
T
TEEN AGE 13+
© TACHIBANA HIGUCHI / Hakusensha, Inc.

.hack//G.U.+™

"The World" as it's never been seen before!

In the three years since the events of *.hack//Legend of the Twilight,* The World has become The World R:2...a dangerous game overrun by player killers and where lawlessness abounds. Follow Haseo as he chases Tri-Edge and gets involved with Project G.U. and the mysterious AIDA that plague The World R:2!

FOR MORE INFORMATION VISIT: WWW.TOKYOPOP.COM